NO FIXED ABODE

NO FIXED ABODE

The **Life** and **Times** of
AMERICA'S GREATEST
UNKNOWN SPYWRITER

James Atlee Phillips

FORT WORTH, TEXAS

Copyright ©2025 by Liam Phillips

Library of Congress Cataloging-in-Publication Data

Names: Atlee, Philip, 1915-1991 author.

Title: No fixed abode : the life and times of America's greatest unknown spywriter / James Atlee Philips.

Description: Fort Worth : TCU Press, 2025. | Includes bibliographical references. | Summary: "No Fixed Abode is a memoir that reads like a novel. James Young Phillips, AKA Philip Atlee-his pen name-was the rebellious scion of Texas country club nobility whose first novel, the highly praised The Inheritors, was compared to Hemingway and scandalized the Fort Worth social scene to such a degree that it was banned from the city's library shelves. From his reckless youth in Fort Worth to World War II adventures on bullet-strafed Chinese airfields, a tempestuous marriage to a runaway Swedish baroness, and his creation of fictional super-spy Joe Gall, America's hard-nosed answer to James Bond, Phillip's life story just might offend, and even outrage-but will certainly entertain"— Provided by publisher.

Identifiers: LCCN 2024049844 (print) | LCCN 2024049845 (ebook) | ISBN 9780875659107 (paperback) | ISBN 9780875659244 (ebook)

Subjects: LCSH: Atlee, Philip, 1915-1991. | Authors, American—20th century--Biography. | LCGFT: Autobiographies.

Classification: LCC PS3501.T56 Z46 2025 (print) | LCC PS3501.T56 (ebook) | DDC 813.54 [B]—dc23/eng/20241126

LC record available at https://lccn.loc.gov/2024049844

LC ebook record available at https://lccn.loc.gov/2024049845

TCU Box 298300
Fort Worth, Texas 76129
www.tcupress.com

Design by Preston Thomas, Cadence Design Studio

CONTENTS

Preface   vii

Part One   **THE WASTREL YEARS**   1

Part Two   **THE WAR YEARS**   83

Part Three   **THE WANDER YEARS**   157

Acknowledgments   249

Bibliography   251

About the Author   256

PREFACE

ONCE, IN A BRIEF BUBBLE IN TIME, four Phillips brothers emerged from the middle-class country club society of Fort Worth, Texas. Sons of a corporate lawyer who died young of the dollar fever, they strutted briefly in the mid-twentieth century.

David Atlee Phillips, the youngest, became the best known internationally. In World War Two he bailed out of a burning bomber over Austria and was a German prisoner of war for a year. While running an English-language newspaper in Chile, he hooked up with the CIA and became a high-ranking spymaster.

Olcott Phillips, number three in the quartet, enlisted early in World War Two and trained for the conflict using trucks to simulate tanks and wooden sticks as rifles. While still a private, he refused to lecture his company on military intelligence on the grounds there was no such thing. Out of boredom he turned to boxing, won the heavyweight championship of the 36th Division, and went to the Golden Gloves national finals. Then of course the military intelligence rushed him to officer's school.

The third brother, James Atlee Phillips, was a much-traveled writer. He showed great promise at an early age, and at seventy-five continues to show great promise. Many acres of trees have been destroyed to allow him the dubious validity of print.

The senior Phillips brother, Edwin, was a pleasant lawyer practicing by himself. He emanated a false camaraderie and had all the usual fraternal connections but was essentially a loner, vainly trying to emulate the distinguished father who had founded a large firm. Earlier he had fought a respectable World War Two, slogging through New Guinea as a captain in the Signal Corps, and wound up in Tokyo in the Judge Advocate General's branch. While his three brothers attracted public attention one way or another, he maintained his small law office and read the *New York Times*, the *Journal of Commerce*, the *Guardian* (when it was still published in Manchester), and all the news magazines. Of the latter group he thought *The Economist* best.

I never glimpsed the precision of his mind until after he was fifty years old. During a brief visit to Fort Worth, I was regaling him with my recent travels through Africa when he corrected me on the distance between Djibouti and Aden.

We were in the study of his home. He got us another beer, asked me to stop spewing bullshit for twenty minutes, switched on his desk lamp, and went to work on some poster board. Half an hour later he flipped me a freehand map of the African continent. Every national boundary and large city was labeled and larger topographical features were included—the Rift Valley, volcanoes, deserts. I checked especially the Nile River. He had indicated its two sources. My favorite port in Africa, Lourenco Marques, he showed as Maputo, and that change was recent. What astonished me most was the way he showed proportionate sizes, whether of river systems or mountain ranges. After comparing his hastily drawn map with the one in the atlas, I told him it was remarkable.

Then it occurred to me that I might have chosen an area in which he specialized. I asked him to render me another map, this

The Phillips Brothers, left to right: David, Olcott, Jim, and Edwin. *(Author Collection)*

one of southeast Asia. I had run a military charter airline there during Burma's civil revolt. Now I requested that he define the Shan states and their border with China.

That took nearly an hour, but the result had the same meticulous balance. National boundaries were exact, although the Indo-China peninsula looked too long. He had even indicated the opium drug-routes which later were called the Golden Triangle. I checked his drawing against the atlas again and asked why he hadn't become a cartographer.

Edwin laughed, steepled the *namaste* sign at me with both hands, and uncapped another Mexican beer. "More than one way to see the world, Jimbo. You guys go rushing out to gape at foreign real estate, marveling at what history has done, and I sit here in my little hidey-hole and chart what history did last night."

PART ONE
THE WASTREL YEARS

I LEARNED THE SOCIAL VALUE of deceit early from my older brother, Edwin, when I was fourteen. We were the top layer of the four Phillips brothers, aged eighteen down to twelve. Our father, an affluent corporate lawyer in Texas, had died suddenly three years before, at the age of thirty-seven. My mother, named Mary Louise but called 'Maryllis' by her friends and family, was trying to bring us up under certain stringent rules.

The most inviolate of these rules was that we had to check in with her every night after returning home. The hour of our returning had nothing to do with the ceremony, and there were no exceptions. Even if it was dawn, we had to knock on her upstairs bedroom door and say good-night before stumbling to our own beds.

Eddie-katz and I roomed together. He was a high school senior preparing to attend the University of Texas, and fancied himself as a master of highlife and imbibing. On the night that made history in our family, I had awakened and seen by the clock it was past 4:00 a.m. Eddie's bed, next to mine, was still made up.

Listening in the darkness, I heard the car roar into the driveway at what seemed an unreasonable speed and thought it might go right on through the garage and roll onto the golf course. The door to the garage went sliding shut and I heard his uncertain passage through the kitchen and lower hallway.

He came groping up the stairs slowly. I could visualize him regrouping on the top landing. Seconds ticked by as I listened, and finally there was a brisk rap on mother's bedroom door.

"Yes?" Her reply was muffled, drowsy.

"Just checking in, Edwin," he whispered. "It's Mother. G'night."

I was transfixed in my bed. Seconds ticked by. Finally Maryllis said good-night, and he came tiptoeing around to our bedroom like a cartoon cat. With an air of great satisfaction, he fell onto the bed beside me and went to sleep in his clothes.

The next afternoon, a Sunday, while we were driving to Forest Park to play in a high school fraternity football game, I mentioned that he had put the big pot in the little one. There had been considerable merriment at the breakfast table, especially by the two younger brothers, about the transition of identities. Mother had tried to smother the glee but was unable to sustain a stern approach.

Eddie was attempting to drive and settle his shoulder pads. "You think so, huh?" His glance at me was contemptuous. "Jimbo, you're a dumb bastard. Remember, I pleated a fender last week, and Friday night I came in sloshed and took out part of the hedge."

I nodded. It was true. But I didn't see what bearing these things had on the matter.

"So I was feeling no pain last night and figured to get grounded for at least a week. This way we get an amusing family anecdote, and maybe my ass won't be grass after all. If everybody just keeps on smiling, maybe I'm home free."

I stared at him with mounting awe and thought he would probably become a fine lawyer.

AT AGE FIFTEEN I enrolled in the University of Texas at Austin. This was a lineal progression. My father had been a tackle there, my mother was a graduate, and my older brother, Edwin, was a pre-law student.

Eddie regarded my precocity with controlled disgust and felt he was being used as a babysitter. We shared a room in the house of Professor Ramsey, an engineering teacher, and the strains in our relationship deepened. Eddie was a high-minded type, but he had one habit for which I could not make an allowance. At dances he got quietly drunk and led the band, with sweeping gestures, hair in his eyes, and mindless rapture on his face.

There were other impediments to peaceful coexistence. I was too young to buy cigarettes, and he always had plenty but refused to share, claiming our mother had so instructed him. That meant I had to scrounge constantly. His smokes were safe from pilfering because he kept them locked in a tin box which held two cartons. We had kitchen privileges, and one day I took his precious tin box and baked it for three hours in the Ramseys' oven.

The cigarettes were Lucky Strikes, or had been. Their publicized motto at the time was They're Toasted. After my heat treatment the residue was not even snuff.

By arrangement, our laundry was picked up once a week by a friendly Black woman and returned two days later. For some reason I have now forgotten, the return was once delayed. Since I had a tennis session coming up and needed my whites, I went to the laundress's home. She was not there, but her nubile daughter gave me the clean clothes and, after an appraising glance, suggested that for another dollar we could have a match.

We went through some high-spirited acrobatics on the worn couch. After my tennis match, while showering, I had sudden qualms about our impromptu union. I was not necessarily a dummy. The thought of a dread venereal that could cause my gonads to drop off seemed a real danger, so I searched the medicine cabinet for a suitable disinfectant. The only thing that seemed likely was a bottle of Lysol.

I doused my member full-strength with the dark fluid. It felt reassuringly cool. We went to sleep early in our twin beds because we had eight-o'clocks the next morning. After an hour I levitated smartly, scrambled into my corduroys, and took off toward Seton Infirmary across the campus.

A young doctor listened to my groaning story and silently administered first aid. It took awhile. When my impromptu dance had diminished to a trembling shudder, he stated that anybody who would subject his own crown jewels to such treatment should be under constant observation, like in a nut hatch.

"Unfortunately," he concluded, "you will not lose your penis. In a few days a cracking process will take place on the encrustation, and eventually your manhood will emerge again. You will have a lovely pink dick. Come in tomorrow afternoon and have the dressing changed."

You can't keep a good Christian down, not if his heart is pure. For the next week I crabbed cautiously around the campus, never missing a class. Eddie monitored my erratic progress and antiseptic smell with a stoic eye but never asked a question. He didn't want to know.

MY AMATORY WOUND was healed by the time spring pledge-rush began. Both my parents had belonged to Greek-letter societies, so Eddie and I were on the pledge lists. We went to various houses to drink gin and be entertained, swam at Barton Springs, and joined midnight blanket parties, pairing off with sorority gigglers.

Eddie and I were inevitably thrown together on many of these occasions, and he threatened me with early death if I got smashed and made fools of us both. I tried to use moderation in all things, but there was an inevitable reckoning. A grim committee from the Interfraternity Council came calling on Eddie and announced that I had pledged six different fraternities. These young bloods, who took their undergraduate world seriously, maintained I had made a mockery of the selection process.

When the outraged committee departed, Eddie offered the opinion that I qualified for world-class asshole and was ruining his career to become a big man on campus. I thought of mentioning his idiot Toscanini act before dance bands but decided that would not help.

I improvised, saying that all the rush parties had been enjoyable and that there were arguments for every fraternity. This maddened him further.

"We'll concede," he said, "that you may really be that stupid or irresponsible. But included in your acceptances was Sigma Alpha Mu, the only Jewish club on the campus."

"Yes," I answered, "but they were the most intelligent bunch of all. Among other things, they've got a lock on the *Daily Texan* staff and the lit magazine editorships. Maybe," I suggested, "*we* are Jewish."

"Possible," he said wearily, "although I don't see how. The name could be derived from Phillipowski, I guess. Our maternal grandfather was a star cotton-broker who was also alcoholic. Dad's father came into Texas ahead of the MKT railroad. Directly ahead of it, laying track. Did his drinking under the Baptist banner."

We pondered the possible permutations.

IF MY GRASP ON FAMILY antecedents seemed vague, it was because my father had not been a player for several years. Horatio Alger gone upscale, he was a blond giant who had played tackle at the University of Texas and been a semi-pro baseball catcher. While siring four sons, he had run his law firm into a mini-conglomerate with offices in several cities, employing ninety-odd barristers.

My memories of him were limited. I remembered his physical presence and booming laughter in the new home on the golf course as he shot craps on the living room rug with the chairmen of various boards, corporate nabobs from Stone & Webster, Cities Service, Freuff Trucks, and Montgomery Ward. My sharpest memory was playing hardball catch on the lawn, where from a crouch he snapped the ball back so hard it turned me halfway around and left me with a stinging palm. He laughed at me, exhorting: "C'mon, boy! C'mon, boy!"

His timing, like his meteoric rise to affluence, was perfect. After going through a complete physical at Scott-White Clinic he was pronounced in top condition. Three days later he walked off the third green, across the road and into the house, and passed me without comment. I was reading on a couch in the hall. Two days later he was dead of lobar pneumonia, at the age of thirty-seven, no antibiotics then being available.

From the windows of the upstairs dormitory in the new house, his four sons watched the long funeral procession haul him away. The oldest boy, Eddie, was fifteen. I was next, and Olcott and David completed the roster. The occasion was muted, and we were suitably saddened because that seemed the keynote of what was happening. It was several years before we realized that he had died of that deadly American disease, the dollar-aristocracy virus—a malady of the wealthy elite that I would later describe in my first novel, *The Inheritors*: "Patient men who had been so strongly indoctrinated with the virus of the dollar aristocracy that they could not

Edwin Phillips, Sr., Born January 9th, 1890; Died September 5th, 1928. A well-respected lawyer rumored to have played a part in founding the Rivercrest Country Club. *(Author Collection)*

enjoy themselves even when they were financially able to do so." Pneumonia had merely killed him. It was the dollar-aristocracy virus that had done him in.

If he had lived another decade, and moved his firm out of the

Mary Louise Phillips, known as 'Maryllis,' became an active member of the Ft. Worth School Board after her husband Edwin Phillips's death. Mary Louise Phillips Elementary School in Ft. Worth is named after her. *(Author Collection)*

1929 shadow, he would undoubtedly have become a tycoon. Sixty years later, widely scattered oil and gas interests he took as contingency fees are still producing revenue. His choices for long-range investments were remarkably sound, but many had to be dropped because my mother found herself unable to carry them all. Not with four sons.

We were by no means destitute. The sons were fed, housed, and educated. They became fixtures in their country-club Christian society and set about creating definitive karmas, some of them singular.

DURING THE SUMMER MONTHS, those of us who found golf too slow formed a tennis brigade. We often played a dozen sets, lunging and shouting in the heat. Our play was not technically very good because we made every shot a "kill" attempt. Still, it was a way to pass time, and after a swim in the club pool we were ready for that night's serious drinking.

One of our comrades was a laughing, pleasant boy called Beavo. His father was a well-known lawyer, and his grandfather was a rich entrepreneur with a gamey image. One day I was to pick Beavo up at noon on my way to the tennis courts. When I arrived at his house I found him downstairs in his father's study. With him was a stocky, unfamiliar fellow who had not come to play tennis.

His name was Danny Robinette, and he had a Cajun accent. We shook hands perfunctorily, and I wondered what the hell he was doing in Beavo's house. Because Robinette was unlike my fellow wastrels. He dressed and talked like a pirogue guide and still had the bark on him.

The two of them had been considering some records scattered on the desk. Beavo began putting them away. The local scuttlebutt was that he worked part-time for his notorious grandfather, but he had never brought the subject up in conversation. The way he played, drank, and disturbed the night air with us, he couldn't have worked very hard at such a job.

"That's it, then," said Robinette as we started out of the house. "You get the money off, and we'll meet in Baton Rouge when everything's set."

"Right," answered Beavo. I had the impression he hadn't wanted me to meet the brusque little Cajun. But if that was true, why had he asked me to pick him up?

"You cats plotting against the whites, are you?" I inquired jokingly.

Robinette was putting on a frayed straw hat. He stopped and turned to me. "You must be the bleeding heart who writes poetry.

No, sir. We're plotting *for* the whites, and we're runnin' late."

"Oh?"

"Bet your country-club ass, cousin. We're putting the finishing touches on a little campaign." He thumbed his nose. "You familiar with Baton Rouge?" I nodded. He pronounced it "Bat*on* Rouge." "And when we pull the trigger, the nice folks who live there will wake up one mornin' to find a prominent Jew businessman hanged from every street-corner light in town."

I didn't comment, and Beavo didn't add anything. Robinette strutted out to a battered pickup truck parked in front of the house, got in it, waved, and drove away.

Beavo and I went to the courts and had our usual slam-bang workout. As I rocked up to serve the Slazenger ball, I wondered how many street-corner posts there were in Baton Rouge.

Later that night, while drunk, I discussed the project briefly with Beavo, telling him I thought it was disgusting. He winced, reached for the bottle, and said his grandfather paid him five hundred dollars a month to keep records and edit a monthly racist hate sheet. He emphasized that it was mostly proofreading, and that my eyes would bug out if I ever saw a list of the movement's contributors.

A year later I saw a news release about his grandfather's offer to a leading military school in the south. He would donate fifty million dollars to the prestigious school if it would incorporate his white-supremacy theories into its curriculum. The school refused. On a related note, my wife's father was a noted orthopedic surgeon, and by chance I found that for several years he had donated considerable sums to the racist politician Gerald L. K. Smith, as had most of his associates.

The subject of Beavo's part-time job never came up again. In the society in which I grew up in the '30s, Jews were not a subject of much discussion, although most houses in the better suburbs had restrictions in their deeds against Jewish ownership.

THE FACT THAT MY FRIENDS and I formed a tiny aberrant group in the society of Fort Worth was not unusual. Entering the third decade of the twentieth century, we had counterparts in every town of the area, the inheritors of the country-club Christian ethic. We were taught the wrong things, and any attempt at original thinking was viewed as a childish flaw, which would be speedily corrected by the rules of the marketplace. It was denied by our peers that it was desirable to build a sound bridge or a rain-tight house with manual labor. To consider human suffering, individual dignity, or essential fairness as worthy preoccupations was frivolous.

My hometown was subject to two forces which I did not recognize until much later. Fort Worth was at the edge of the great plains, and their population had only begun to shift toward the cities. Dallas, our close neighbor, was off and running early, guided by entrepreneurial Jews and newly rich oil men. Therefore it soon became metropolitan while Fort Worth lagged. We had many of the great ranch families, which later became swept into the oil drilling program, and two of the biggest national meat packers had huge plants in Fort Worth.

The second major force affecting every part of Texas, and national life, was the creation of the Communist menace. This was to remain the great bogeyman determining US foreign policy until now. Herbert Hoover had been a successful engineer but a disastrous political leader. He wrote that if he had one goal in his life, it was to destroy the evil Communist empire. After the capitalist system broke down in 1929, it was useful to have a devil so convenient. Ronald Reagan, who came close to being retarded, was still using it with conspicuous success. It took our minds off our real problems.

AFTER MY AWESOME FIRST semester at the University of Texas, it was decided that the only way to keep me from becoming the uncontested village idiot was to put me someplace where there wasn't even a village. I became an oil scout for Uncle G., a senior partner in my late father's law firm. He and several other partners were honorary uncles to the four Phillips boys my dad had left behind.

The job title was nonsense. I knew nothing of oil or geology, but that absurdity was matched by the fact that my wages were also nonsensical. I lived alone in a small shack in East Texas with no electricity or water. That meant illumination by kerosene lamp and humping in food and water from a farmhouse about half a mile away. For a latrine I had a large stretch of piney woods.

My duties were to patrol on foot all the nearby producing wells, try and estimate their production, and filch what the facts or prospects were on drilling wells. This was difficult because most drill sites were "tight," their crews instructed not to allow strangers on the lease.

The great East Texas oil field had been opened less than two years before, and the discovery well, Daisy Bradford #1, was on my daily route. Although he was not yet known, H. L. Hunt, the Arkansas gambler, was in the great flood of lease-brokers and land men searching for their fortunes in the huge new field.

The somnolence of such sleeping towns as Longview, Tyler, and Gladewater had been shattered. Their courthouses were crawling with major company representatives, brokers, and con men. In many cases these categories were the same. Clusters of Black inhabitants who had lived in poverty for decades were invaded by fast-talking types who offered them unbelievable prices for orchards and cemeteries. They would even unearth the dead and transport them to fine new locations.

In most nations of the world, the title to minerals is vested in the state. Almost alone, the United States included it in the surface title. If you owned the poorest dirt farm, the oil underneath it was included.

I was shipped into this brawling, bustling boom in June of 1931 and made weekly reports on what I could ferret out on the ground to Uncle G. in Fort Worth. Even in my lonely shack, far removed from the fleshpots, it was an impressive pageant. In those days, the rush was for crude oil. Natural gas was important, of course, because it propelled the dark liquid from its underground strata, but after it had done that, there was only local use of the gas. As a result, it was flared off into the air at a corner away from the well and ignited. Some of these flares were a hundred feet high, enormous candles snapping and swaying over the piney woods of East Texas.

They were factors in my scouting because from the size and velocity of the tall flames a rough estimate could be made of the amount of crude being taken out by the well. And every commercial well completed was wide open because the great American depression was paralyzing the nation's economy. East Texas was such a rich pool, widening daily at its edges, that the sudden influx of its crude knocked the market price down cruelly. One well-known oil man was offering to deliver three million barrels of oil for ten cents a barrel.

Two months after I arrived in the field, I was making my rounds of the leases one afternoon when I encountered uniformed Texas National Guardsmen. While I watched, their officer tacked a placard onto a brace of the wooden derrick. They waved at me, got back in their truck and moved on down the back country lane to the next producing well.

The placard was a proclamation signed by the Honorable Ross Sterling, Governor of Texas, and stated that martial law was in effect and that all oil production in the state was now subject to proration rules being established by the Railroad Commission, which would set production limits, to be enforced by law. Until such legal limits had been determined, all wells were to be shut down.

That night there were no more towering tongues of flame over East Texas. They had all been extinguished.

The only thing that made the scouting job tolerable was weekending in Longview. The law firm my father founded had a house-office there which was supervised by C., a prematurely white-haired young lawyer who was an admirable role model for a growing boy. He drank heavily, whored moderately, and handled so much petroleum-related litigation that he became a recognized expert in that field.

Every Friday afternoon I walked or hitched rides to Longview and stayed in one of the bedrooms behind the offices there. The town, like Tyler and Gladewater, was crawling with boomtown followers. C. and I played tennis and explored the burgeoning vice possibilities. The apex of these was Mattie's Ballroom, a barn and group of cabins deep in the piney woods. Dancing, drinks, and the latest in social diseases were on tap at Mattie's.

C., whom I called the Silver Fox because of his white hair, came from a small Texas town and had worked his way through law school in Austin. He had been a Rhodes Scholar candidate but was flatfooted. That fact had knocked him out of the "fully rounded" category. He was a keen observer and told me about noted lawyers he had observed.

One of his anecdotes was about my late father. Dutch Phillips had tangled frequently with a certain judge. In the heat of courtroom exchanges, the judge had fined him five hundred dollars for contempt of court. "Your Honor," the big blond man snarled, "five hundred dollars will not begin to express my contempt for this court!"

The judge banged his gavel down. "How about one thousand dollars' worth of contempt? Would that be closer?"

My father considered, then nodded. "Yes, Your Honor, that would be about right." A dollar was worth a lot more then.

A FIRM YOUNG VOICE rang out over the hushed auditorium with passionate conviction. The teen-aged speaker paused, gestured angrily, and gave his remarks a big finish.

"So, we announce here now, to every scheming munitions maker and corrupt politician, the slaughter is over! Something new is moving forward, something that will wreck the unctuous preachers and commercial patriots. The trumpets are crumpled, gentlemen, and the drumheads are smashed. We won't go to your senseless wars anymore!"

He walked briskly off the stage to mounting applause. He had been addressing a university student body. Some were standing, and a few ripped out cowboy yips.

The year was 1935, the school was Texas Christian University, and I was the speaker. The occasion was the Gough Oratorical Contest. In an hour I was declared the winner and presented with a scrolled gold medal.

The Gough was far from my first victory. I was a local *wunderkind*. At age nine I had had a poem published in the *Houston Post*, and I was a competitor in tennis and swimming meets at Rivercrest Country Club. A few weeks before my TCU victory I had won a divisional contest for North Texas in extemporaneous speaking. In that one, to bolster the belief that I was destiny's tot, I received divine assistance.

The event had been held in an old redstone Methodist Church on a stormy night. I was the last speaker and knew it would take an extra effort because the competition had been good. As I launched into my closing minute, a tremendous clap of thunder erupted and all the lights in the church went out.

Without missing a beat, in the darkness, I summed up my cogent arguments. The judges' meeting was brief. It was obvious that I was a cowlicked youth for all weathers. Indeed, many of the ladies present believed that I was a phenomenon, and I encouraged this belief whenever possible.

Several days later, while in a class, I was notified to report to the dean's office. He was a brisk academic, surveying his fiefdom through thick spectacles. After congratulating me on winning the Gough contest, he took me into the main hall of the administration building and pointed out the massive display case where university trophies were kept. They included several all-American players and two national football championships. Davey O'Brien and Slingin' Sammy Baugh were among the alumni greats.

"As you are aware, Phillips," he informed me, "your medal will join this goodly company on permanent display. No rush, of course, but if you will bring it in next week . . ."

That posed a problem. "Thought I got to keep it."

The dean chuckled. "You do, lad. You do. After you win it twice more. Three times retires it."

We had a major tenet in my family, a hard rule: *The truth if it kills.* When we were back in the dean's office, I unloaded the dumpster.

I told him that on the morning after I had won the gold medal, it had passed routinely over the counter of my friendly pawnbroker on Main Street. An examination with his loupe, a scratch to verify gold content, and he had given me forty-three dollars cash.

This information removed the civility from the dean's face. "Get it back!" he snapped.

"Can't be done. I didn't hock it, I sold it to him. Gone to Melt City by now."

He stared at me as I completed the story. There was a racetrack called Arlington Downs that operated between Fort Worth and Dallas. Buoyed by a tip from a stable hand, I had put forty dollars on the nose of a filly named Two-Slipper. When I got my mutual tickets, she was 18-to-1 and the post parade was on.

Draped on the infield fence, nipping on a pint of Town Tavern, I cheered as the maiden filly broke on top. She increased her lead and was ten lengths ahead, flying alone down the stretch, when she crossed her front legs, cartwheeled to a sickening splayed halt, and was destroyed on the track.

This sad event explained, I said, why I could return neither the trophy nor its cash equivalent.

The dean's expression had gone from exasperation to distaste. Mister Chips seemed to be having stomach pains. He wiped the thick spectacles. When I started to add something he murmured, "Go." As I left, he was still motionless, head down.

FRIENDS OF MY PERSUASION, irritants to the fat society in which they lived, were a tight-knit coterie of pseudo-intellectuals. Our only strength was that we belonged to the society level we were trying to subvert, and as long as we didn't do any real damage, they suffered our posturings.

R. was the most interesting of this iconoclastic group. He was an extraordinarily handsome boy who affected a constant air of scorn, as though the whole world smelled bad. He sported a supercilious curl of lip. He lived in a large mausoleum of a house, which contained life-sized marble statues. His invariable response to almost any comment was, "Rooster's ass?"

R. was important to my formative years because (a) he nearly got me thrown in jail on a serious charge, and (b) when I penetrated his patrician snobbery, a strange new dimension of sexuality opened before me.

R. had a brother-in-law named Harvey, and one night on the prowl we crashed a party at his house. All the guests were in their thirties, winging it on bootleg spirits. (Yes, Virginia, it was once illegal to buy either beer or spirits in the United States. For that reason, nearly everybody was drinking far more than they wanted to.)

Nearly all of us had tried marijuana but it was not much liked. We could buy a Prince Albert can of six or seven "roaches" for a dollar in the Black section of Lake Como but decided that the pungent smoke only made us sleepy and comatose. Years later, working on the Chinese national airline, I met mandarin elders, scholars, and wealthy merchants who smoked opium pipes nightly as part of their regular schedules. They often lived to be eighty or ninety.

The celebrants represented the upper crust in our village. Several of the women were post-debutantes, and the men were lawyers, corporate officers, and political aspirants backed by wealthy families. There were no Hispanics or Jews among them, and the only Black person was a matronly lady supervising the kitchen.

Vitality was supplied by punch from a huge crystal bowl. The ingredients were straight ethyl alcohol and grapefruit juice. At the beginning of the '30s that society was remarkably drug-free except for prescribed barbiturates. You could have shaken the whole crowd down without finding a spike. That was still the hidden province of drug fiends, people in dark alleys. Cocaine was known but not much used, except by showoffs who called it nose candy.

R. and I were there, as always, on a treasure hunt. We were perpetually broke but could usually scavenge a few bottles or dollars after the party got to rolling. Normally we had dependable business channels. If someone we knew wanted gasoline, we could charge it to our family accounts and discount it for cash. The same was true of new suits, groceries, or other goods for which our families had credit. On this particular night, however, we were in one of those dreary periods when all charge accounts had been closed.

Harvey, R.'s brother-in-law, was a cotton broker, an affable blond man. He came wandering by to ask how we were doing. I told him we were doing great and that another glass of his punch would have us barking like foxes and walking up the wall. He got us two more punches. R. said we were going out to Lake Worth to join another party on the Terrells' cabin cruiser. Harvey's face grew reflective.

"Good night for it," he said, and shook his inebriated head. He and R.'s beautiful sister had a lakeside lodge. "Keep payin' taxes on that damned place . . . almost never use it. Be a mercy if the sunavabitch burned down." Sighing, he moved to rejoin his guests.

"Hey!" I called after him." How much would it be worth to us if the damned place did burn down?"

"Unhhh ... about twelve thousand dollars." His tone was jocular.

Three hours later, only a smoking chimney marked the ruins of the lakeside lodge. R. and I were rudely awakened the following noon with the news, which we received with suitable shock. Neither of us had any eyebrows. They had been burned off by the sudden *whuff* of flame as the ethyl-gas-soaked timbers of the camp ignited. R. had insisted on the best grade of gasoline.

People who only a few hours ago had been sporting outrageously, filled with merry quips, now began to come down with stomach cramps. R. and I met in the grill room of the country club and decided to go low-key and make no money demands of Harvey until he had received the insurance money. Sure, there would be a stink, but didn't we have our twenty-one eyewitnesses lined up?

Crime may pay for some people but in this case arson didn't. It seems that Harvey owned only half the destroyed camp. The other half belonged to his partner in Houston, a gentleman we had never heard of. He flew to Fort Worth, looked things over, and announced that he hadn't wanted his half torched and was having a word with the district attorney.

Lawyers met, my mother surveyed me with sorrow, and my older brother, Eddie, said he would like to trade me in for a leper. To further narrow the target, R. quietly boarded a plane for Los Angeles and remained there for several years. He was a good athlete and had even performed hippodrome horse-jumps in the local rodeos, so he was a natural for B-picture oaters and made several of them.

One of the senior members in my deceased father's law firm called me in and remarked that my dead parent would not have been pleased with my conduct. I expressed contrition and signed notes for $3700, made out to Harvey's partner. Whether they were ever paid off or not, I can't say.

THE REPORT THUS FAR on our young white boy seeking to evaluate his world is not exactly spellbinding. The immediate conclusion from his early antics was that we had here an arrogant poseur and smart-aleck scofflaw.

But even poseurs must have something to justify the act. I had several things, one of them being that I was a passable poet. An oil field collection called *The Metal Forest* had been entered in the Yale competition for younger poets. It placed second. One of the judges, Stephen Vincent Benet, had written me a note saying that he had thought it was the best but had been outvoted.

The usual atmospheric sketches, facile but plotless, had been published in regional and collegiate journals. The pieces had a somber view but the occasional felicitous phrase indicated promise if the writer ever grew up. The two largest national magazines that published fiction were *The Saturday Evening Post* and *Collier's*, and after studying them I had stories published in both before my twenty-fifth birthday. It was mostly a matter of what to leave out: no profanity, no sex, no toilets flushing. I was also a competent athlete, member of a state junior doubles tennis championship team, and adept in swimming and basketball.

A novel, *The Inheritors*, was underway and would be published by Dial Press in 1940. The book was an examination of country-club Christianity, the progress of a privileged set of rebels trying to avoid the trap beginning to close on them. In it was my growing apprehension that society didn't work in human terms. The poor, Black, and ill sections could not receive fair and equal treatment when there was so much emphasis on the sufferings of whites and those wealthy elites afflicted by the dollar-aristocracy virus.

That's the case so far for the protagonist. He was ridiculous and immoderate, but he was also questioning.

The simple, understated cover belied the piercing roman à clef tale that filled the pages of Phillips' first novel. *(Author Collection)*

THE COUNTRY CLUB TENNIS courts were not very good. Bounces off the asphalt were erratic, but to compensate for them we learned quick reflexes. Summer mornings we played ten or twelve sets. The afternoons were mostly spent at the swimming pool, and the nights were dedicated to valiant drinking and the pursuit of perfumed quiff.

Lacking instruction, we were free to perfect our bad habits. What evolved from that was a slamming, attacking game, even to second serves. When pursued in competition, this smash-and-volley game means few rallies. If you're "on," you blow the opposition away. When you're missing, you look amateurish.

A friend named Bill Landreth and I evolved into a junior doubles team, and just for laughs entered a local Amateur Athletic Federation tournament. We won it without losing a set and automatically became Fort Worth's junior doubles entry in the state tournament. Landreth was considerably more polished as a player, but together we made a good slam-bang team.

Ed Landreth, Bill's father, was a prominent West Texas oil man who lived across the golf course from us. He was a tanned, affable wildcatter who had beaten the enormous odds against that nomadic tribe and had more patience than any of the other parents I knew.

That year's TAAF tournament was being held in Waco. Bill and I drove down in one of his dad's cars. We were probably the least-experienced team in the junior doubles, but we stormed through the first two rounds, got a bye, and were slated to meet the team from El Paso in the finals.

We approached that match with considerable trepidation since the El Pasoans were ranked nationally. On the morning of the finals, Bill's dad called to say he was driving down from Fort Worth and to wish us well.

That made the cheese more binding, because we had an uncomfortable secret. When we were kneeling beside the court, ready to begin, we both searched the stands but could not spot Mr. Landreth. "Okay," murmured Bill, "here goes nothing."

We won the toss, Bill served, and we won the first game. Without finesse or moderation, smashing lobs, volleys, and even half-volleys, we kept stepping up the tempo. No letup on second serves—they got slammed too, and went in like they had eyes. Our opponents grew grim and methodical, trying to fight back our unorthodox blitz with blocks, slices, and drop shots. It didn't work. Chalk spurted from the lines as everything we hit went in. We took them in straight sets, and as we accepted the trophy and left the court, we were still looking for Bill's dad.

Later we sat in the hotel coffee shop and waited. A beige Lincoln finally parked in front of the hotel, and Landreth Senior got out. He walked into the lobby, consulted the desk, entered the coffee shop where we were sitting, slapped us both on the back, and ordered a club sandwich.

Haltingly, Bill told him how we had been drinking beer the night before and the road had suddenly become treacherous under us. The beer was to blame. It tasted like fusel oil. In short, the new Plymouth had been smashed and was even now resting in a rocky gully with its tires in the air.

"That a fact?" Mr. Landreth's mouth twitched. "But both of you are all right?"

"Dad," said Bill, "we won a tennis tournament a couple of hours ago."

His father's smile returned. "By God, you did." He beckoned for the waiter, who went to fetch an assistant manager. After getting the location of the wrecked car from us, Landreth issued brief instructions. Then he turned to his club sandwich, and between bites had us replay the match for him.

The oil man was one of the few acceptable role models I had met. I filed his conduct in my mind.

MY VANTAGE POINT, from a medium-sized city at the edge of the plains, was sharply limited. Valid conclusions could only be reached by talking to those seeking the same goals. Perhaps then there would be revelations.

My approach was agnostic, the gospel which produces the only true believers. I had from birth heard the unctuous zeal of the Baptist roaring in his pulpit and seen the Roman priest flouncing in his gaudy ball gowns. *Jesus's Daddy gonna git you if you don't do right!* This eternal din never stopped, exhorting me to heed fables invented by a carpenter's son who had left no history and no artifact in his brief sojourn among us.

I would go find out, observing on foreign corners the muezzin chanting from his minaret, the sadhu mumbling enlightenment along dusty roads, and would chat with the great heads on Easter Island. A reflective man might even sit under the great bo tree where Lord Gautama meditated his sermons.

I would preserve, or even add to, my own icons. That meant walking through the threatening twilight of El Greco's *View of Toledo*, wading through the surf at Dover Beach to observe ignorant armies clashing by night.

Searching for clues to the perfectibility of mankind.

BOYS EMERGING FROM PUBERTY have one major concern: the love gland and where to put it. At first they find their own hands satisfactory. Masturbation has undeniable advantages. It relieves sexual tension, is private, and you don't have to get dressed to do it.

But the male hand is not really the proper sheath for the penis. It belongs in the vagina, and when the dancing begins, pheromones begin to inflame the quivering nose.

Allowances would always be made. Most of the girls we wanted would not put out. Some would suck, most would indulge in mutual masturbation, a few would allow anal insertion. Since I pored through medical texts, I understood early what went where, but few of my generation received dispassionate charts of the journey through the fever swamp.

The one aspect of sexuality which remained unclear to most of us was homosexuality. I had read Krafft-Ebing, Sacher-Masoch, and de Sade, and pondered the axiom that there was only the true inversion, determined by prenatal factors. How to explain to the school of overpowering maternal influence which vitiated the paternal bond? The macho element seemed to crumble before Fierce Mama's attention.

I tried to equate what I read and what I saw around me. After my global journeys began, I saw young men walking hand-in-hand in many Asian cities and had to admit that their attention to each other was based on simple economics. In impoverished societies, men could not afford to pay the dues of female courtship.

The matter seemed important. I was attempting to become a scholar and, if possible, an artist, and the record showed that a tremendous percentage of great creative artists all through history had been homosexual. Was their sensitivity arising out of a refusal to accept the domination of the vagina?

These were my conjectures. In conversation with my peers I fell easily into the mandatory macho ribaldry. The childish snickers were endless.

ALTHOUGH I WAS THE CHIEF instigator of our rebellious coterie, R. was a remote, vitriolic eminence. He was so darkly handsome that girls locked on immediately. He had been a member of the Black Horse Troop at Culver and was an excellent horseman. When he was eighteen, as a professional performer, he had hippodrome-jumped a pair of horses at our annual Fort Worth rodeo which, with Calgary, is one of the best in the world.

What interested me was that while R. joined our badinage and could squire any girl he wanted to ask out, he never joined the double-dating parties in which two couples drove into the woods and coupled on blankets in the darkness. In our personal relationship there was never the slightest irregularity. He had no feminine characteristics.

When our relationship was interrupted by the impromptu fire at H.'s lodge, he flew to the West Coast before the angry litigants had even lined up, and I did not see him for nine years. I received news, of course, and occasionally the late, drunken telephone call. He was appearing in B westerns and even got featured in a short series.

When I did see him next, I had just checked into the Town House in Los Angeles. John Wayne's producer at Batjac, Bob Fellows, had picked me up at the airport. Batjac, Wayne's company, was interested in the possibility of making a movie out of *Pagoda*, a novel I had recently published. My first phone call in the suite was from R. In half an hour he swaggered in.

He was still Apollo-handsome but life in Hollywood had begun to yank him out of shape. He was full of nervous twitches, and when I asked him how it was going he answered, "Pussy good," still with the scornful curl of lip.

Since I wasn't due to meet Wayne until noon the next day, R. and I made a quick tour of the city. I disliked it then and still do, so we cut it short after an hour at Lucy's and returned to the suite. More serious drinking ensued—straight sour-mash, water chaser—and R. showed me what seemed like hundreds of theatrical glossies taken during his cowboy career. He got solid drunk, started sprinkling his talk with "Rooster's ass?" again, and spent an hour ripping me up and down as being an interloper.

The gist of his tirade was the unfairness of life. He had spent years getting in to see producers and directors, inferring that often he had been subjected to unbearable humiliations, while I just sauntered in for a chat with Wayne, who had recently been on the cover of *Time* magazine. I didn't know fuck-all about the screen or writing for it, and those rodeo stories of mine he had read in *Collier's* were pure bullshit anyway. It seems I didn't have a clue about anything.

"Not even payin' for this fuckin' suite, are you?" he inquired.

I said no. Batjac was picking up my expenses.

In earlier days I would have needled him deftly, saying that peons had to take it slowly while quality folks always arrived at the front door on the cuff. But there would have been no joy in it. The way he had drunk himself into a sullen rage made me wonder how he could stay on a horse or deliver lines to the camera.

I ordered dinner from room service, but he only picked at his food while still belting away at the Jack Daniel's. At midnight I told him I was tucking it in and he was welcome to use the other bedroom. Did he want me to order him a toothbrush?

"Rooster's ass?" he replied, reaching for another drink.

My bourbon torpor was disturbed some time later by an erotic dream. Hands or a mouth or both were working my genitals. I thrashed upright in the darkened bedroom. R. reached again, but I evaded him without difficulty. When I had led him to the other bedroom, I returned to mine and locked the door.

Now, forty years later, as AIDS reports fill the daily press, I wonder if R. made it.

WHEN THE LADY I WAS RIDING threw me off the bed a second time, I realized it was no preliminary bout. We had been at our carnal frolic for nearly an hour. I was recently turned eighteen and in good shape, or so I thought. My opponent, a trim, poised woman of uncertain age but gargantuan desires, watched me climb off the floor and approach the bed again. We were both glistening from the film of oil she had applied from an expensive *flacon*.

Motioning me to immobility, she poured us another pony of chilled Bols gin. Then she carefully replaced the little glasses on the bedside table, gave me her vertical smile, leaned back and murmured, "Onward."

We had been at this contest for four afternoons, and the pace was beginning to tell on young Jimble.

I had met this insatiable appetite the previous Sunday afternoon, through my mother, at a garden wedding. We had arrived early at the afternoon nuptials, held at one of the mansions across the golf course. The long garden was manicured, a tribute to topiary art, and huge trees cast pools of shadow as the guests and principals circulated prior to the actual ceremony. A string ensemble hidden on the terrace above sent lively airs across the sward.

The ladies wore long dresses in pastel colors and wide-brimmed hats. (Where have all the big hats gone? To join the cloches, one by one?) Inevitably I met many people I knew, or knew of, and was introduced to several new ones. One of them was Mrs. T., who had recently moved to our town from the East. She was tall and, while not beautiful, was making the most of what she had, by which I mean a good figure. I automatically made her age at the late forties. When I started on, following my mother, Mrs. T. stopped me with a white-gloved hand.

"You're a poet, I hear," she said.

"Aspiring to be one, yes."

"Ahh . . . I'm interested. I have been an editor. Could I see your work?"

Her tone was interested. She had stopped gossiping.

"I'd be flattered, if you have the time."

"Tomorrow afternoon I have the time. If you'll bring your work, I'll give you a drink."

I nodded. "See you then."

As my mother and I walked home after the wedding, twilight was deepening over the pond hazard on the fifth hole. I told her about the invitation from Mrs. T. Mother, well aware of my dislike for culture vultures, hesitated before replying.

"Might be interesting. She's quite sophisticated, I hear. Spent several years in Paris, knew Hemingway, Stein, that crowd."

My interest in Mrs. T. heightened. If she had rambled through the arrondissements with Joyce, Fitzgerald, and Stein . . . Ezra Pound was the one who interested me most. The Pisan Cantos were yet to come and his anti-Semitism had not yet filtered back to our hinterland, but he seemed to be helpful to all his friends and was said to have edited Eliot's *The Waste Land*, sharpening it enormously.

"I'll bet she knows, or her friends do, every big literary agent in New York," I said. Eventually I would need an agent for the novel I was sweating over.

"Probably," agreed my mother. "Your best behavior, please, so she won't think us benighted savages in Cowtown, so far from Athens."

MRS. T.'S HOUSE, LIKE OURS, was across the street from the fifth fairway. Scrubbed and looking like an Episcopalian choir boy, with my poetic output in the manila folder under my arm, I knocked and was admitted. The Black maid showed me into a sitting room where Mrs. T. was waiting.

We chatted idly for a few minutes, and she asked if she could see the work. I handed it over. Before opening the folder she pressed a button on the side-table beside her chair and the maid brought in a tray, glasses, and an ice bucket cradling a bottle of Bols gin.

I watched as she poured two drinks of chilled gin. I was feeling defensive, as all fledgling writers do when approaching a verdict on their private sentiments by a stranger.

I need not have worried. Mrs. T. read several poems silently, making short but relevant comments on my outstanding gaucheries. Then she reached for a large book on the side-table and handed it to me, saying I might like to look through it while she was examining the rest of my poems.

I opened the large book, expensively bound in red Moroccan leather, and nearly came out of my Queen Anne chair. With my peers I had snickered over the Tilly books, which delineated the sexual adventures of an errant secretary. What now confronted me in both photographs and drawings by skilled artists was the entire gamut of things erotic which could be done with every aperture of the human body. This book must have come from the private collection of J. P. Morgan or some English nobleman. My neck grew warm at the astonishing displays.

I finished my gin, and Mrs. T. looked up from her reading to pour two more. Beyond the drawn blinds I heard distant calls from golfers going by across the street. When I had finished my third drink, Mrs. T. closed the folder which held my work, which was no longer relevant, and stood up. I followed her obediently, up the stairs and into the master bedroom.

My days fell into a pattern. I had a noon class every day at TCU. When it was over, her car would be waiting at the northern edge of the campus.

The third afternoon I donned a deerstalker cap as we approached the bed, explaining that we might not be in the same county at the end of our workout. Mrs. T. thought this mildly amusing. On Friday afternoon of that first week we were writhing as usual when a voice from the doorway of the bedroom said "Pardon" apologetically.

Mrs. T. paused, leaned against the headboard, and raked hair away from her forehead. A dapper little man standing in the doorway said he had just flown in and didn't know she was busy. She swept him out of sight with an imperious hand wave, and we resumed our calisthenics.

I never saw the polite little man again but presumed it had been her husband. He seemed a tolerant sort. My mother had told me he was an executive in one of The Seven Sisters international oil companies, but Mrs. T. never commented on his brief appearance.

My work as a persevering stud was bearing tangible results. She had written letters of introduction for me to several literary agents in New York. She was flying out to her house in Santa Fe, New Mexico, the day after my school term ended, and I was to ferry her Buick out there so that we could spend the summer together.

I had a key to her car, and she had given me four hundred dollars cash to cover traveling expenses. This was satisfactory because I could make the drive nonstop, and my expenses would be less than fifty dollars.

My mother was a tall, slender woman, called Maryllis by her friends. Her patrician face was in somber repose when she awakened me at three a.m. on the getaway day, the day I had planned to drive Mrs. T.'s Buick to Santa Fe. Final exams had gone well, and my intention was to arise at noon and take the drive easily. I had not announced this to anyone because I didn't need another brouhaha.

Half asleep, I stared at her as she stood beside my bed. My older brother, Edwin, was a motionless mound in the next bed.

"Get dressed," instructed my mother quietly, "and come downstairs for breakfast."

Breakfast? At three a.m.? "What the hell is—"

"Now," she added, and walked out of the room. I went to the bathroom and splashed cold water in my face. My toothbrush was gone.

Downstairs in the kitchen, breakfast was waiting. As I sat down to it, my mother poured herself a cup of coffee and sat down opposite me.

"Your artistic progress is accelerating too fast," she announced, "so we have changed the plans. When you finish breakfast, I will drive you down to the Greyhound bus station. Your ticket will take you to Odessa, Texas, where they have an oil field. Until you return to school next September, you will be employed by Gulf Oil as a roustabout at a pay of $7.04 a day."

"Sounds idyllic," I said.

She nodded, unsmiling. "You have a room reserved in Mr. Dunn's boarding house. I have returned Mrs. T.'s four hundred dollars, so you can return that amount to me now."

I fumbled out my wallet and removed the wad of bills in it. "Thirty-something bucks short. We partied a little last night."

She took the currency, went upstairs to dress, and we drove downtown in darkness to the bus station. My gang foreman's name was Shorty Meyers, and I would report to him immediately after I had checked in at Dunn's boarding house. She handed me a twenty-dollar bill and a bus ticket. As the Greyhound belched out of the station going west, she watched from her parked car.

IN THE BACK END OF A TRUCK with eight other grimy hulks in overalls and steel-toed, high-topped shoes, I meditated on the surgical precision with which my mother had converted a rising scholar to serfdom. The dictionary definitions of roustabout include some categories with romantic connotations. Hustling canvas up in the circus, chaffing clowns ogling high-wire ballerinas, preparing for the calliope's tootling calls. Dock workers swarming over cargo off seagoing vessels. My category came last, an unskilled laborer in oil fields.

Still, if you are young and can get through the first shock of hustling heavy pipe, cranking and uncranking it by the numbers, brushing mesquite off truck routes to drilling rigs, and mucking odorous residue sludge out of oil tanks being dismantled or moved, your constitution will adapt to it.

I even found the specific remedy for a hangover. Under direct 100-degree sunlight, spend eight hours with a sledgehammer, driving metal posts to fence in a drilling area. Sweat rimes your shirt white, and even your toenails perspire freely. Attention must stay concentrated since a fellow roustabout is holding the metal post erect while you swing at it, and he will be vexed if you miss.

During those initial days while the neglected body learns to accommodate, you perform like an automaton, to survive. If you manage that, the other gang members slowly note differences in speech, philosophy, and work effort. Which ones are malingering so that pipelining can become a threat to safety. If they ride down on the tongs at the wrong time, destroying the rhythm, you can damage knuckles or break hands.

As my vision cleared, I began to notice particularly a tall lantern-jawed boy named Buster Dixon. Buster was even younger than I was, probably seventeen. He knew the routines of our work well, since his father was a veteran rig builder, and he had learned how much effort to expend on any given task. Buster was so ignorant that he seemed almost simpleminded. That was obviously because he had never been to even a small city. But he was curious. He wanted to know about the world beyond the *llano estacado*, the staked plains of Texas.

One afternoon the collar-pecker, the man who set the rhythm for the tongs screwing the pipe into place, had just rattled us off a completed joint when I noticed that Buster was pacing along toward the next joint in an odd attitude. Shoulders held back and hips thrust forward, he was urinating an arching yellow stream. I had never seen this common act performed with such brio. After about nine steps, the precise fan of piss stopped abruptly, and Buster snapped his lower torso back and brought his shoulders forward. His feet were in the precise place for cranking the next joint of pipe.

That put him opposite me in the tong line. While the stabber was lining up the next length of pipe, I asked Buster why he did it that way. He hitched at worn cotton gloves.

"This company," he stated, "is working me like a mule and paying me like a mule, so I might as well piss like a mule."

"In motion?"

"Fuckin' A."

Riding back into town at quitting time, hands dangling between my knees, I meditated on his small act of rebellion. Eight of us were seated, four opposed, in the dark truck cabin, and when a foul odor defeated the permanent stench of crude oil and sweat, one of the lowered heads said, without malice, "Some dirty dog has crept in and crapped," and another voice added, "Wish the bastard would creep right out."

It seemed to me that Buster had solved an old problem. Most men, all their adult lives, fight a losing fight against the last drop of urine. Since they generally perform the act from an upright position, many attempt small gavottes or sweeping turns to loose the ultimate drop from the spigot. Women, crouching, were not so subject to the drainage problem. Gravity solved it all. Buster Dixon, it seemed to me, had resolved this universal complaint. He unloaded his liquids from a moving platform.

After a week of roustabouting my muscles began to adapt to the heavy work, and I decided to teach Buster Dixon how to speak Russian. This was an enormous task because I knew no Russian myself beyond *da* and *nyet*. But it seemed to me Buster was ready to expand his horizons. A true son of the plains, at age seventeen he was already over six feet tall. Splayfooted, wearing bleached bib overalls, with a shaven head which looked like a Bartlett pear, he had never visited a town larger than Amarillo, in the Texas Panhandle.

He had heard Robbie, the gang pusher, kidding me about being a brain because of my meager writing credits, and knew I had been to two universities. All of us carried our lunches to work in tin boxes, and one day I invited Buster to join me in the shadows under a pipe rack. As we settled down in the dry loamy dust I informed him that he must learn Russian; that he had the credentials for being a leader of the people and must begin to prepare for that role.

"Gah!" said Buster.

[I reminded him that] the name of his hometown had been chosen by Russian railroad construction workers in honor of the original Odessa, in Russia. And our version of the name was in almost the exact center of the Permian Basin, one of the great oil pools. It was only a part of the huge geological system which mantled all continents and was named for the province of Perm, near the Ural Mountains. The Permian System had been laid down over two hundred million years ago, in the Paleozoic era, and contained several petroleum pay zones.

"Gah!" repeated Buster. His admiration was deserved because these facts were true. He had wolfed down his sandwiches and was gnashing into his white onion, always his dessert of our noonday meal.

I said that American intelligence had received word that the Russians would try to take over the northwest part of Texas, including the Big Bend area and the Panhandle, because of the huge oil deposits in the region.

"Bullshit!" commented Buster.

"Listen, boy, don't make up your mind until you hear all the facts," I admonished him, adding that we were wide open for invasion all along the Rio Grande, with nothing to bar intruders but "bobbed-wire" fences. I claimed that, by the terms of its admission to the United States, Texas had the right to split into four extra states. If saboteurs with unlimited funds infiltrated from Mexico and created separate states across the *llano estacado*, what would happen to the huge oil pool?

Before Robbie banged on the water cooler to call us back to work, Dixon was working on his first Russian nouns. I made them polysyllabic, guttural, and explosive, and they came trippingly off Buster's tongue like epiglottal barks.

Buster Dixon's vigil had begun. He scouted the town and roamed the leases on his days off, all the way to the Mexican border. He sat in on Odessa civic meetings, surveyed crowds at ball games, snooped around tourist courts. In the weeks that followed I would be bending over my stick, squinting at pool balls, when a nasal whisper would come from the shadows beyond the clacking "moon" tables.

"*Gospodin?*" That would be Buster, point man of the new frontier, reporting on his latest surveillance.

CARL BABCOCK WAS A FEISTY bantam gamecock from Drumright, Oklahoma. A tight-wound little man, he was the collar-pecker on our pipeline gang, rattling out tong rhythms with a ballpeen hammer.

In such work there is a "stabber" who, from the far end, makes sure that new joints of pipe are properly started before the tongs start turning them. If the male, inserted end is cross-threaded into the female socket, the joint cannot be cranked in. And when a clumsy stabber did his job improperly, Carl would growl in disgust: "I bet if you put hair around it, the dumb bastard could find it."

The company had a full-time pipeline crew, but they were professionals and worked the miles of pipe across leases. Our work was only local connections at tank farms and pumping stations. Carl knew his job and performed it with dispatch, but he didn't have good sense.

Off work he was a heavy drinker and took offense at almost anything. That attitude got him poleaxed, lacerated, and whittled on. When I joined the roustabout gang, Robbie, the pusher, told me to avoid him because he was trouble.

His latest exploit had taken place only a week before I arrived. Babcock had gotten into a fight arising from a dispute at the dice table in the Silver Slipper night club. In the ensuing free-for-all, he and a notorious local character named Gomez had duked it out until a switchblade had scalloped Carl's face and forearms. Gomez had been arrested and indicted and was awaiting trial.

Most people of modest intelligence would have been thankful to avoid serious injury and waited for justice to take its course. Not Carl. Before his slash wounds had healed, he spent hours in the lockup wing of the Federal building where Gomez was incarcerated. Carl would curse his assailant and spit through the bars at him. He knew several sheriff's deputies, and through them gained access to the cell tier.

I was told that the Mexican brigand had laughed at his antics at first, then had become hydrophobic at the sight of Carl, shouting and clawing through the bars. Once he seemed to have learned patience and was sitting motionless on his bunk when Babcock pressed forward to taunt him. Leaping forward, Gomez drenched Carl with the contents of his slop jar. This low blow caused the indignant Babcock to complain, and Gomez's slop jar was removed from the cell. Like so many passing vignettes, I never knew the outcome of this one because my own life began to feel some ill winds.

ALL MY LIFE I HAVE BEEN a foe of patriots and nationalism because I think the two qualities have caused more carnage than religion. Yet, at a few times in my life, I have been proud of the citizen company I kept.

After my roustabout gang finished its day, we were driven from the headquarters lease into town, being dropped off at our various destinations. We rode in the back end of a truck, lined on each side by wooden benches. One day the truck was being loaded for the trip to town when an office honcho came running out of the superintendent's office.

The weather was bad and getting worse, ominous dark clouds rolling in from the north, accompanied by rising gale winds. The man from the office stood leaning in the back doorway to the truck's cabin. The seated roustabouts could see angry lightning forking out of the clouds looming over the endless prairies. Thunder cracked so loudly it seemed the earth must be splitting.

We could not hear his first words. Then, in a lull from the storm, the message came: " . . . School bus lost. . . . hours overdue, North Ector County . . . accepting volunteers to grid search . . . "

The heads of the seated roustabouts, topped by greasy hats and caps, considered the intruder. Their reaction time was short. All hands went up automatically and we filed, groaning, back out of the truck.

As a young, stridently vocal liberal, I had often joined my peers in castigating the major oil companies. Their profit-enhancing depletion allowance, their efficient lobbies both in Washington, DC, and Texas, with unlimited funds to spend.

As stormy twilight deepened around the little oil town in West Texas, winds increased and the forward visibility lessened. The problem was not economics or politics. It was much simpler than those amorphous entities. Seventeen schoolchildren were lost, their school bus unreported, in the storm.

The municipal police force and the sheriff's department of Ector County were composed of amiable dullards, few in number. The state highway patrol could not assemble troopers fast enough to mount a decent search. But one call to Gulf lease headquarters could do it.

Everybody volunteered. Off-duty field workers began arriving in strength, flowing in from houses and bunkhouses. Drilling rigs were shut down so that drillers and tool dressers could join the search. One by one, trucks were given routes. Two went out to the state highway which the school bus had used, and others were assigned farm-to-market side roads off that highway.

Most tool pushers and administrative men drove company pickups. They rocketed back and forth to check on the searching trucks, pinpointed on the map at headquarters. That was their only connection. They had no radio, and the cranky local telephone service was patchy from blown-down poles and wires snapped by windborne debris.

The storm rolling across the great plains was called a blue norther, or a blizzard. These weather phenomena usually blew from southwest to northeast and incubated whirling winds that formed "Tornado Alley" further east and through Oklahoma and Arkansas.

The land men and geologists manned the war map with colored pushpins. It was a natural assignment, because they had initially surveyed every acre of it. They knew every access road to the leases' tank farms and drilling and pumping well locations.

My own participation was not heroic. Our truck worked through the storming darkness with almost no forward visibility for several hours. We veered slowly off the highway on side roads, following the school bus's itinerary. When these rough tracks petered out, we had to grope down fence lines to check out lonely farmhouses and isolated pumpers' shacks.

After two hours of this impromptu groping search, the two

hundred-odd men involved had checked every home where the seventeen schoolchildren were to have been dropped off. At midnight there was still no report of the big orange bus.

The unsmiling men at the headquarters map never paused. They were methodically eliminating places the bus could be. When it became obvious that it was nowhere on its normal route, they sent the fleet back out, rerouting the searching trucks beyond the normal range to points it could have possibly reached reached in error.

The principal concern was the thought that if the school bus had run out of gas, it could no longer operate its heaters. Temperatures in the raging blizzard were dropping rapidly toward freezing. Our truck had been recalled to the headquarters yard, and at around one a.m. we were being handed out boxed meals and hot coffee, eating inside the back cab. A pickup came roaring into the pipe-yard and slewed around behind us. Even over the storm blast we heard the pickup's shocks being punished by the tubular cattle guard.

The tool pusher ran into the brightly lit office, and we heard a ragged cheer go up. Robbie, our boss, went jogging toward the welcome sound and came back grinning like a brush-ape.

"That stupid driver wandered all the way up to the Johnson-Whitlock, nearly out of Ector County. But we got seventeen young 'uns, all safe. They were gettin' frost-bit, but everybody's fine."

WHEN MY PERSONAL TROUBLE CAME, it had blonde hair and was named Thelma McFarland. Her father was a mud salesman—not ditch-water mud but a specialized type used in drilling, to wall off natural gas and water—and had a bad temper. He had allowed me to date his plump daughter only after investigating my antecedents and had promised to stomp my asshole into a mudhole if she came to harm. There was no Mrs. M. to contend with. She had taken it on the heel-and-toe with a derrick man in Deming, New Mexico, some years earlier.

The spot chosen for our revels was the notorious Silver Slipper club outside town. It was a low wooden structure painted blue, with a crap table in the back room. Silver dollars were used as a wagering unit instead of chips, and the few winners staggered off on the bias from the weight of their increment. I had bought a new white shawl-collared jacket and lace dress shirt for the occasion, and was so deeply tanned that I must have looked like an Anglo-Saxon Indian. Thelma had managed to get nearly all the way into a low-cut bodice and a bouffant skirt.

Two friends from the roustabout gang and their wives were seated with us at the table, and they were similarly slicked up. In Odessa, this was high society.

The place was jammed. The five-piece band blared with more enthusiasm than skill. Thelma and I dipped and swirled to "Smoke Gets in Your Eyes" with so much bodily contact that she made me return to the table to unfasten the gardenia corsage I had sent her, which was in danger of being tattered. The levels of the Seagram Seven bottles dropped steadily.

By midnight I had beat the back room for over fifty silver dollars and backed away from the table. That was enough to pay for the whole evening's frolic and show some change. On the way back to the dance floor, carrying my weighted coat over one arm, I passed by a large table in the back. Inadvertently, the skirt of my trailing coat brushed across the edge of the table and upset several drinks in tall glasses. Two of them rolled off the table and shattered on the floor. I wiped moisture off my new coat and apologized, admitting it was my fault and saying I would pay for the drinks. There were six people sitting around the table. Five of them looked at the big swarthy Greek at the far end. I had heard of him. He was a Greek named Nick Z.

"Not that easy, Jack," he announced with a smile. "You will go get us six fresh drinks. You will do it personally."

I had upset only three drinks and offered to replace them. The Greek was pushing. I reached into the inside pocket of my coat and took a twenty-dollar bill from my wallet, dropped the bank note on the table, and said, "That ought to cover it."

I was back at my own table, telling Thelma about my luck at the dice table, when my chair went flying backwards with me in it. From the floor I saw Z. staring down, his feet planted apart. From my angle, he looked like the Colossus of Rhodes.

"Outside," he said, jerking a thumb toward the parking lot. As I pushed up from the littered floor he started toward the far door, circling the dancers. There were many things I would rather have done than follow him. The Greek had been second-team All-Conference guard at Texas Tech a few years ago. He was now a tool dresser for Shell.

As I followed him toward the door, the music stopped. I tried to remember what our feisty collar-pecker had told me. *Always protect your eyes and teeth. If you're outmatched, rush him and throw him your best punch. If nothing happens, take an artistic dive.* Thelma, tearful, tried to pull me back, but I kept walking toward the parking lot.

The crowd was humming, emptying the dance floor. When I got through them, Z. was waiting. He had his coat off and was holding it. With a sigh I stopped and started to peel out of my own white jacket. When I had it back to my elbows, pinioning my elbows, the Greek swung his own coat with both hands and clubbed me over the head. I dropped like a poleaxed steer as his winnings sluiced out of his makeshift bludgeon. He had obviously won more silver dollars than I had, but Marquess of Queensbury was not imprinted on any of them.

Consciousness returned several hours later in the small Midland hospital. Thelma and her father were staring at my bandaged head from across the quiet room, and a doctor was explaining that I had a concussion. Eleven stitches had closed the wound over my right eye, but I would probably retain the sight of it.

The doctor said the McFarlands could visit for five minutes. After he had left, Thelma's father said Sheriff Dickey would be in to see me about noon. Then they left, Thelma throwing a kiss. She was almost radiant. It had obviously been a big night for her. Cautiously, I tested the wrappings around my skull.

Two days later, preparing to check out of the hospital, I had a visitor I didn't expect. From the way my mother had railroaded me out of the orgy circuit to join the day-laborer set, I had thought that I would receive a visit from some member of my family, or at least an inquiry when I got maimed while waltzing with strangers. My mother obviously had a direct connection with Gulf headquarters in Fort Worth, and they must certainly have informed her of my mishap.

My unexpected visitor was not a family member but Nick Z. He entered the hospital while I was getting my stuff together.

"Come to finish me off?"

"No, man, nothin' like that. I appreciate your not bringing any charges with the sheriff's office."

"What the hell for? I was smashed to the gills and knocked your drinks over. Your reaction was a little brisk, however."

"Why I'm here." The Greek spread his big hands, stared down

at them. "After I got out of school I tried to do a little pro boxing. You know, pick up a little moolah flattening stiffs. Well, all I managed was to break up the knuckles on both hands. Can't punch my way out of a paper bag anymore. That's why I had to sandbag you."

I nodded, and he turned and walked out. I pondered briefly on Samson shorn of his best weapons, then checked out of the hospital and got in the company pickup which would take me back to the Odessa boarding house, where I would recuperate until it was time to have my stitches removed.

MY ROOM AT THE BOARDING HOUSE was more like a stall, one of many in a shed-like row which flanked the main house. In my partitioned section there was a straight-backed wooden chair, an iron cot, and a bare light bulb dangling overhead. Clothes hooks screwed into the wallboard beside my small mirror completed the West Texas Gothic decor.

Their steel-toed work shoes were the most valuable item many of the resident laborers owned. They often slept with the cot's iron legs pinning down the shoes.

After I arrived from the hospital I sat on the cot for a couple of hours, making notes, jotting down ideas for oil field poems or short stories. These meditations were interrupted by trips to the smaller, more pungent structure at the end of the long room-shed. I had diarrhea, probably induced by the sanitary food at the Midland hospital. Inspiration is always fleeting, and it suffers when interrupted by unplanned dashes to the cesspit.

My head hurt even after I had gulped down the painkillers, and I kept wanting to scratch the stitched area over my eye. Sometime before midnight I switched off the light and tried to sleep. As I was drifting off, there were mounting sounds of altercation from the adjoining cubicle. Angry shouts, grunts, and muffled thumpings, followed by the shattering of glass.

That fight was spirited. Howls of mindless profanity, more thrashings that shook the floor and walls, and a cracking sound. A bare back, bowed, broke through the plasterboard wall, knocking my mirror and hanging clothes to the floor. The back vanished, leaving a jagged hole in the wall.

There was another angry spate of threats and profanities, a final exchange of blows punctuated by heavy grunts, and one of the gladiators sat down heavily. I got up and looked through the hole.

The warrior who had stayed home was sitting on the end of his cot, wearing only shorts, taking a drink from a pint bottle. He was short, with heavily muscled shoulders, and was bleeding from the mouth. The focal point, however, was the wrinkled, featherless bird perched on his shoulder. It was larger than a chicken and pinker than a baby. I had the startling thought that perhaps all its feathers had been knocked off in battle.

The warrior in repose must have heard me, although he could not have seen me. Looking at the hole in the wall, he said, "Evenin'."

"Right," I answered. "What's that?"

"Eagle. Young 'un. We was tearin' down an old wood derrick on the Scoville lease. Found him in a nest, top of the derrick."

The naked eagle didn't look very imperial. The bloody-chinned man on whose shoulder he was shifting and cawing said that he was going to train him up for "huntin', like they do with hawks." Seems the man was swamper on a Landreth truck, and his fight had been with its driver. He didn't say what had caused it.

When I snapped on my own light, he in turn stared through the hole at my bandaged head but did not remark on it. He did say he was sorry about the hole but I told him it didn't matter, no real harm done. In another fifteen minutes he had finished the pint, turned off his own light, and was snoring heavily.

My head still hurt so I had another painkiller. I was faintly angry, wondering why the hell I hadn't heard from my family. Was it that they just didn't give a damn? Was I like the absurd eaglet, being trained to hunt the hard way?

Sitting in the midnight darkness with the little oil town sleeping around me, I tried to remember my goals but was not even sure I could define my purposes. All I knew was that what I sought was not to be found in Odessa, Texas. This wasn't the place.

THE NEXT MORNING, before eight o'clock, I was awakened by one of the Mexican maids from the Dunn dining room. "*Telefono*," she said.

It was my mother, calling from Fort Worth. "Jimbo," she said crisply, "I love you very much, but you must be the biggest fool God ever made."

"Possibly," I answered.

"Do you have full vision in that left eye?"

"Yes, ma'am."

"Fine. This afternoon you will get the stitches removed at the Midland hospital, then catch the bus to Fort Worth. In September you will enter the University of Missouri at Columbia. Your transcript is already there. You cannot enter the Journalism School until midterm because you are deficient in a math requirement. It must be made up. Any questions?"

"Yes. How the hell are you, anyway?"

Her laughter, well remembered, came down the line as she filled me in on conditions at home. After we had hung up I walked back to my stall to pack, realizing for the first time what the Greeks meant when they created the *deus ex machina*.

THERE IS A BIG UNIVERSITY at Columbia, but I called it Coventry. I was there on strict probation and lean funds. The riotous days of wine and roses were now verboten. One more ill-considered Dionysian revel with jug and gas and property damage, and my search for higher education would be over.

Naturally I found the campus and everything on it a drag. There were few exceptions. My original interest in the school was based on the presence of Walter Williams, who had founded the journalism school and made it the best in the world. Attending it was denied me because of a few lacking hours in math. I lived in a room off campus and soldiered along to make them up.

There were a few bright spots. Work on my first novel was proceeding, and I was encouraged by an English lit professor named Ainsworth, a remarkably perceptive teacher. That made two I had been lucky enough to encounter. Lorraine Sherley at Texas Christian University, who had instigated my first novel, remains the finest editor I have encountered after publishing thirty-four books.

One of my clearest recollections of the University of Missouri was yellow snow. Football fever was a virus at the school, and the weather toward the end of each season's schedule was severe. During the break at half-time I saw a sight new to me. Thousands of male students stood in long ranks, facing away from the stadium, and pissed into the drifts. The toilets under the stands were packed and odorous, with long lines forming, so most male students chose the more aesthetic form. When play resumed, they left long yellow and orange slashes behind, which would have delighted Van Gogh.

The Shack was a major attraction at the campus's edge, a beer joint that was always crowded. Anyone willing to buy the occasional round could hook into a festive group. Since among other pursuits I was forbidden to enter a Greek-letter house, these impromptu circles at The Shack were my point of entry into Missouri society. Often, with my Texas twang, I seemed to be consorting with foreigners, so thick around me were eastern seaboard accents.

Bob Wertz was a law student. Nearly bald, bespectacled and intense, he constantly sought ways to embarrass the Establishment. He lived in Sioux City, Iowa, and asked me to drive him to the bus station so that he could go home for the Christmas holidays. Since thousands of students were flooding out of Columbia for the same reason, the lines at the ticket windows were long.

Wertz avoided this delay by giving a student near the head of one line ten dollars to buy his ticket. When he started to board the bus to Iowa I was directly behind him, carrying his bags. But there were no seats. He could board, the bus driver told him, but would have to stand in the aisle. Wertz stared at him and shook his bald head.

"That," he announced, "is your rosy-red ass, friend."

Turning, bulling his way back through the boarding line, he ordered me to put his bags in the front of the bus and sit on them. On the ground, just ahead of the big wheels. All of a sudden we had a project, but I seemed to be the designated patsy. If those wheels turned, it wouldn't be Wertz under them.

He waved my protests away and charged into the bus station. Sitting on the bags, I watched a minor crisis build. Departure time came and went. Arriving buses were stacking up on the streets outside the station. The local police ordered me to move. Wertz came charging out of the station and bulldozed into them. He stated specific violations of Federal and Missouri law, giving subsection numbers. The ticket he had bought entitled him to—nay, assured him of—a seat to Sioux City. If bus personnel or police laid a hand on him or on me, his agent, they would be subject to severe litigation on several counts. Swinging his arms, he quoted a number of cases as precedent.

The crowd had grown enormously. Wertz enlisted a student with a camera to wait until "these Cossacks" laid a hand on us, then freeze the infamy on film.

After a delay of over an hour, the bus company put Wertz and three other students into a taxi and sent them toward Sioux City, while hundreds cheered.

While at the University of Missouri, I was neither an instigator nor inciter. During one prolonged session at the Pennant Hotel I somehow got hooked up with a group from Mount Vernon, New York. One of them was a heavy-shouldered Italian boy who had failed as a quarterback, and two of them were obviously of Irish descent. Five in all, and to me they all talked funny. After several hours of beer-drinking and lying to each other, we took off for the campus in two cars.

I was asked to carry a small bag and, since it wasn't heavy, obliged. As our little group skulked across the quiet midnight campus, I asked one of the Irish guys what the deal was.

"We're going to blow up the columns," he whispered.

"Pardon?"

"We're going to flatten the columns in the quad."

"Why are we going to do that?"

"Shake the bastards up." He showed me the folded skeins of wire and the blasting cap he was carrying. "You got the dynamite sticks in that bag."

It was too dark to see but I felt inside the bag. There were four stubby lengths inside it, wrapped in greasy paper. I was a merry prankster, feeling no pain, but not yet a total idiot.

Blasting the columns would shake the bastards up, all right. It would shake the Governor of Missouri up, since the weathered columns at the heart of the campus were symbolic of the school. I handed the bag to my accomplice, wheeled, and cut down the nearest side street, chop-chop.

Fortunately, the conspirators began quarreling as they strung the wire, and a campus cop bagged them all. The newspaper report said that their explosive equipment had been stolen from a storage shed on a dam construction site, and that five ex-students were returning to Mount Vernon, New York.

On another Saturday night I was one of a group of celebrants who were joined by a local printer I did not know. He was a tall man in coveralls who specialized in telling jokes. They weren't very funny but were so dirty that it didn't matter much. When The Shack closed, he invited us all to continue our drinking at his house, which adjoined his print shop. After nine of us had crowded into the front room, he waved us into seats and went into the kitchen.

We heard but could not see his wife talking with him. She didn't sound angry at the sudden midnight invasion. Soon he came out with a tray of frosted beer bottles. Jazz music was blaring from the radio, broadcasting from the Black Hawk restaurant in Chicago. We chattered on, our printer host very solicitous, repairing to the kitchen periodically for bowls of nuts, tidbits, and more beer. The woman never appeared.

I was engaged in telling some plausible lies about my heroics in the Texas oil fields when I noticed the printer whispering to a student on a sofa opposite me. The boy looked surprised, then nodded, got up and walked through the right-hand doorway into a dimly lit bedroom. He was greeted by a murmur and the door closed.

In twenty minutes he was back with us, reaching for another beer. Automatically I thought that the printer host was pimping his wife.

Another student returned from the trip into the bedroom. "It's a freebie, man! And she's as hot as a pistol."

I don't know how long a pistol can stay hot, but after the eight other students had gone in to get pussywhipped, it was my turn. I couldn't make it. That many predecessors . . . I passed.

The printer host remained jovial. He flushed us out and invited us back. Any time, he said.

I HAD A HANGOVER. So what else is new? The Pontiac convertible was parked near the clinic entrance, and from it I could see the front doorway, pooled under an overhead light. Few cars were passing. It was nearly midnight. When she had been inside fifty minutes, I crushed out my cigarette, got out of the car, and walked to the clinic entrance.

I stood in the pool of light for another fifteen minutes, then sat down on the top step. When she came out, I arose and took her elbow. Even in Houston's normal muggy weather she was wearing a coat. I wanted out of the carbolic zone, so I pressured her elbow to greater speed across the nearly empty parking lot.

"Don't hurry," she whispered. "I'm bleeding."

In twenty minutes we were back in the room at the Rice Hotel. She went into the bathroom with the small kit they had given her at the clinic, and I had a drink of Virginia Gentleman. She had discarded the cloth coat, flung it over the bed nearest the bathroom, and I noticed a stain on it.

She came out wearing her shorty nightgown, with her makeup renewed, a new paint job to sleep in. I removed the coat, spread the coverlet and sheet back, and tucked her in. As her long legs came up I noticed the loin harness she was wearing.

When I kissed her goodnight, her green eyes raked me from a tense face.

By the time I had downed another drink, she was asleep. I switched off the light by her bed and went into the bathroom. Two transparent medicine containers were still open under the lavatory mirror. Demerol and Nembutal. Her father was a doctor. She always had plenty of everything.

I was hungry but didn't want the blather involved in calling room service. It was my first abortion, and I didn't want any more of them.

ONE SUMMER MORNING IN 1938 I got jailed in Monroe, Louisiana, for defacing a church wall and violating public morals. I stayed locked up for two days because the incident was a scandal to the jaybirds. With the help of a professional bill-poster, I had covered that virginal Baptist wall with a huge, lurid, billboard-size lithograph of a nearly naked cowgirl riding a bucking bronco. The offending sign was pasted on, fixed to the white wooden wall by a quick-drying adhesive. Once set, it became an immovable part of the building and couldn't be washed off, scrubbed off, or steamed off. The type on the gaudy picture boomed the message of the Fort Worth Frontier Centennial Exposition and promised the highest jinks since Sodom.

The following year was the centennial celebration of the state of Texas, and the official show commemorating it was awarded to Dallas. Once again our neighboring city to the east had put us down. In Fort Worth there was the usual grumbling, and Amon Carter, the influential publisher of the *Star-Telegram*, decided that our town would not take it anymore. He called the cowtown's monied aristocrats and told them how we were going to put Dallas in the shade with an unofficial and almost impromptu entertainment festival.

Amon Carter was a tall, frog-faced booster who wore elaborate western garb even in New York's 21 Club and before the crowned heads of Europe. He handed out huge western hats to every celebrity he met. After bulldozing the local moneybags, he called Billy Rose, the diminutive eastern impresario, and hired him to produce, immediately, a Fort Worth festival devoted solely to entertainment. Its motto was to be "Dallas for Education, Fort Worth for Fun."

Rose said no, that there wasn't enough time to mount such a spectacular production, which would cost a mint anyway.

"Wrong!" barked Amon Carter. "Your expenses are unlimited. What would your fee be on that basis?"

"Thousand dollars a day," said Rose. "Minimum of a hundred days."

"Done," said Carter. "I'll fly somebody to New York tomorrow with the contract, and you're on the payroll as soon as you sign."

I knew Amon Carter, of course. Not many people *knew* him, but most everybody who lived in Fort Worth, or Texas, knew *about* him, as you know about a tornado or a plague. My mother had become the head of the industrial development department for the Fort Worth Chamber of Commerce, and through her we followed his eccentric progress.

Once, not long before, I had creased the fender of one of his chauffeur-driven Cadillacs and, because of the insurance problem involved, was sent to his office at the newspaper. Mrs. D., his longtime secretary, asked me to wait a minute in her outer office. Mister Carter, she explained, was about to talk on a long-distance call. While I sat there, she told the White House operator that Mr. Carter was ready to talk to the President. I sat waiting for my thirty-second interview while the publisher chatted with FDR. The gossip was that Amon had turned down several cabinet posts.

What followed Carter's call to Billy Rose was as hectic as the Oklahoma land rush. The little promoter came down with cadres of professional workers—casting director, choreographer, stagehands—and a new direction in spectacle management. Swimming and diving coaches and trainers. The outdoor spectacular and amphitheater they dubbed "Casa Mañana" (House of Tomorrow) was to be both a stage musical and a swimming ballet.

You shouldn't keep something that promising a secret, so ten new Ford trucks were painted red, their sides blazoned with gaudy showgirls clad in wisps, performing as they would in the forthcoming Frontier Centennial show. On each red truck there was a team of two. One was the driver-manager and the other a professional bill-poster. The red fleet fanned out into the states surrounding Texas and pasted and tacked up four times as much paper as Ringling Brothers' Circus. I know because I was in charge of the first truck out.

My duties in the number-one billing car were clearly defined. I was to handle all details regarding maintenance of trucks and lodging of the two-man team aboard it. Most importantly, I was to find the hits. Hits were the places where we could paste up or tack up our gaudy lithographs or posters. The sides of barns exposed to the highways were particularly sought. These locations were paid for, at my discretion, with tickets to the Frontier Centennial show. For an important hit, fifty or even a hundred dollars' worth of tickets was not too much.

This transaction, often with suspicious farmers, was a delicate matter. Our route went up through Oklahoma, over through Arkansas and Tennessee, down through Mississippi and Louisiana. Most of those I bargained with, regarding the proper number of tickets for the site, had a fixed belief that because we billed like a circus we must travel like a circus. There were dates on our signs, but nothing stated that the show went anywhere but Fort Worth, Texas. It didn't, of course, and for years I mused over the fact that thousands of tickets out in the hinterland went unused while their owners waited for the big show to arrive.

We carried three kinds of propaganda in the trucks: billboard-size 32-sheet lithographs, plus nine- and three-sheet cloth banners for smaller locations. They all blazed with bold colors. On my six-state swing I had four bill-posters. Even then they were an endangered species.

I had often heard that painters were heavy drinkers but not until I worked with bill-posters did I learn what a real drinker was. Because our expense accounts dictated that we could rent only one room a night, I also quickly found out that most bill-posters smelled like gut-wagons. All the time. Their imbibing was not showy but constant. They stashed half pints everywhere, and when drought loomed they would sell new hammers, boxes of tacks, anything to replenish their stashes.

On the other hand, bill-posting was an art, so perhaps they drank to concentrate. Their most dreaded enemy was wind. On calm days they could deftly wield that long-handled brush and unfold the gaudy lithographs into place. I think the most awesome sight in nature is a drunken bill-poster hit by a sudden wind gust. He will curse and furl the big sheets of sticky paper in the wrong place, try to correct it and fail, turning and swearing all the time, and finally wind up turning into a flapping, paste-dripping chrysalis of paper. Finally even his legs are imprisoned, and he topples, swearing hoarsely, to the ground.

All is not lost, however. If you watch the lumpy, grounded object, you will see a hand break through the pasted bonds, flourishing a half-pint as it re-enters the cocoon to find the hidden mouth.

Our fleet of red trucks stayed on schedule, however, because the man in charge of billing, Vic W., had superintended the same work for Ringling Brothers and knew every characteristic and scam of the bill-posters' fraternity. Three of them got fired from my truck, but our supply of lithographs and banners was never interrupted.

When I got jailed in Monroe, Louisiana, Vic flew there, greased the right palms, and hired a local carpenter to remove our antic cowgirl sign and put up new siding. What had happened was one of the pitfalls of my job. Looking for good hits, we would canvass the neighborhood until we found someone who claimed ownership of the site. In Monroe, an affable gentleman rocking on a porch assured me he was the responsible party to see about the white wall. In our haste we neglected to notice that the other end of the building was the front end of the Baptist church. Maybe the bogus lessor was a Methodist.

Not even the most talented and meticulous producer can know that a stage show will be memorable. Lively, a commercial success, yes. But to fuse the disparate elements of pacing, visuals, and music so that what has been attempted enters the collective memory of the audience and remains there is a matter beyond planning.

There is one absolute requirement: a featured song which indelibly marks the show. "Casa Mañana" had such a song. "The Night Is Young and You're So Beautiful" by Dana Suesse, a young associate of Rose's whom the papers called "the girl Gershwin," was the climax of the Fort Worth revue. Sung by a Broadway musical mainstay named Everett Marshall to his cloth-of-gold-caparisoned love under the stars of North Texas, it lingers on half a century later, and helped make the show a rousing success.

As rushed as the inception of the show had been, a petulant reaction to the official show in Dallas, it was still the product of show business professionals Rose had hurriedly assembled in Fort Worth. Combining the pageantry of a Broadway musical and a stunning outdoor swimming ballet had never been done before. It was a triumph of serendipity.

AS MY TWENTY-FOURTH BIRTHDAY approached, life seemed to accelerate sharply. I had managed to get through four university years but was unburdened by a degree. My literary career consisted of the odd published poem, some turgid skeins of plotless prose in regional journals, and a collection of oil field poetry titled *The Metal Forest*, which had been privately published. I had a personal record of immoderation in most things and was regarded warily by my peers.

I decided to move to New York. Having spent my apprenticeship in the minor leagues, I was headed for the towering ziggurats of Manhattan, where the money was. Most of those who knew me were delighted. They anticipated an ass-buster on the way to the Hotel Astor.

There was a joke current at the time. A DC-3 approached an airport and landed routinely. From it streamed two hundred Lilliputian figures, smaller than dwarfs. One control-tower operator turned to the other in astonishment and asked, "How the hell can they get that many people in a DC-3?"

"No problem," was the answer. "Those were Texans with all the bullshit squeezed out of them."

The odds were long, but they were no hill for a stepper. I had a job working for Billy Rose, the showman who had produced the Fort Worth Frontier Centennial. He had never seen me and was unaware that I had driven on one of his garish billing trucks through several states. The job had been arranged through my mother.

I had a novel for sale. *The Inheritors* was the usual ego-driven autobiographical tale, told better than most. I had a list of literary agents in New York and knew I would have a better chance for publication by walking into their offices. Otherwise it was a blind shot over the transoms of publishing houses, and manuscripts rarely got picked out of their slush piles.

Though never named directly in the author's manuscript, the author's first wife, referred to as 'Zen,' was Joyce Clayton, the well-to-do daughter of famed Ft. Worth cardiologist Dr. Irvin Clayton. She is seen here modeling for The Fair Store at Rivercrest, 1941. *(Author Collection)*

I had a wife. Zen and I had stood still before a rural justice of the peace long enough to become one. One more problem, her father thought, when I went to his office to break the news. He was a fine orthopedic surgeon whose practice extended into several states, and it was clear from our grim exchange that he wouldn't have minded treating me for multiple fractures.

Still, I did have a job, even if a menial one. I did have a manuscript I liked, and I did have an uncommonly beautiful wife who had already started modeling. And, perhaps best of all, we had a lease on an apartment at 100 West 57th Street in Manhattan, which seemed a natural base from which to conquer New York.

I GOT MY FIRST LOOK at Billy Rose under the sloping seats of the New York State Amphitheater in Flushing, site of the 1939 World's Fair. His Aquacade pageant-revue would turn out to be the principal entertainment feature of the Fair, playing to millions of people at a 99-cent top, two shows a day. The Amphitheater, which he leased from the state, held about twelve thousand, and most of the time was SRO, far above fire department regulations.

Rose had been the subject of much gossip and some controversy in Texas. There were stories of high life in his suite at the elite Fort Worth Club. In one of them, a local beauty being interviewed took offense and threw him over a sofa. That should not have been difficult, since she weighed more than he did. On another occasion he had been eating dinner in a steakhouse with some notables when a local bravo had strapped a Chateaubriand with mushrooms over his head.

He was reviewing the troops when I saw him in Flushing. A hundred-odd young men and boys who would be the ushers and

Following up his success with the Ziegfeld Follies, Broadway impresario Billy Rose opened the glamorous swimming revue known as 'Billy Rose's Aquacade' as a featured attraction of the 1939 New York World's Fair. Undoubtedly the inspiration for 'The Case of the Shivering Chorus Girls.' *(New York Public Library - Public Domain)*

The Aquacade, located in Flushing Meadow Park, Queens, had a pool that was 275 feet long with stands holding 10,000 people. The opening ceremony featured Olympic swimmers Eleanor Holm and 5-time gold medalist Johnny Weissmuller, most famous for playing Tarzan.
(New York Public Library - Public Domain)

floor managers for the front of the house awaited him in rough formation. Among us were college students, aspiring actors, male dancers, and a favored few who had worked on Billy Rose productions before.

Rose's visage was somber as he considered us. He appeared to be about five feet three or four inches. His jaws were bluish, and I later realized that they were that way most of the time. Dark hair was plastered straight back on his skull. He began by remarking, without heat, that the Aquacade was not a snake show. This sounded like carny patois to me. He said the job would be a good one, and we would be playing to people from all over the country. If, however, any of us started knocking down on him, we would depart his employ in some haste because he knew all the scams we did and a few more.

Without showing any emotion he walked away, and his lieutenants marched us off to get measured for blue uniforms.

ZEN AND I quickly settled into the small 57th Street apartment, finding it, for our purposes, the center of Manhattan. Sixth Avenue was directly to the east and the Plaza and Central Park two blocks north. The subway entrance was convenient for my trips to the Flushing show, and she had the requisite hatbox and photograph portfolio for her modeling work. She found lean pickings in fashion photography, and much of the time her attempts to get clothes modeling resulted in the usual "no give, no job" from proprietors in the rag trade. She was poised enough to wave good-bye to such swine.

In our off-hours we roamed Manhattan and took the obligatory ferry trip to Staten Island. The pizzerias, which had not yet become a national eyesore, were a special delight. We were perplexed by the fact that New Yorkers seemed to speak to strangers only when they were enraged by something. They didn't seem to like each other. The natural camaraderie we had grown up knowing in the Southwest was entirely missing. The other floor residents in our apartment building never spoke in passing, even after we had lived there for over a year. On the other hand, there was no danger. You could walk the midnight streets without fear anywhere in Manhattan.

A few days after the Fair opened, Zen called me at the Aquacade just before we were ready to open the doors for the matinee show. She sounded unhappy. She had been in the kitchenette when a tremendous thud had shaken the floor. A suicide had leapt from a high apartment in our building and landed on the roof of the building next door, just outside our bathroom window. Zen murmured that the jumper had been a woman. "She's busted open. Smells like hell."

I told her to call the superintendent's office and report it, then get out of the building. Go to a movie, anywhere. She said she had an appointment in an hour. I told her to go to it, to stay out of the apartment until I met her in the lobby after our night show.

TO A GROWING BOY the '39 World's Fair in Flushing was a continuing delight. Twice a day, we opened the doors of the Aquacade, and the world walked in. Literally. From every state and most foreign countries. There were impressive scientific and technical exhibits, but our show was a fast revue of musical comedy and swimming-and-diving turns that amounted to water ballet.

I was one of several floor managers who supervised the usher corps. The Amphitheater seats and floor had to be cleared of debris between the two shows, and it took quick work. My standard patrol was on the top ramp behind the elaborate control booth. After several weeks I could tell when the show was lagging by a minute or two. The firemen were there, too, because we usually had patrons seated on the stairs and standees clogging the ramps. There was no roof on the Amphitheater, and I often wondered what would happen if we got a sudden storm. Would the house panic?

The performers worked on a standard stage behind a curved lagoon flanked by diving platforms forty feet high, with two springboards below. Skirting this area was a curving walk between the footlights and the swimming tank. Synchronizing the lighting and musical charts in an open-air arena was a staggering problem, but it was routinely supervised by a scholarly genius in the control booth named Carleton Winkler. His disparate elements were a pony chorus line, lofty and statuesque showgirls, the singing principals, a corps of swimmers featuring Olympic gold medalists Johnny Weissmuller and Eleanor Holm, and the astonishing Olympic and clown divers, six of them sometimes flipping and pinwheeling at once.

One summer afternoon, during the matinee show, I noticed from my high perch that the arrogant passage of the showgirls around the front of the ramp was hitting a snag at the center part of their journey. Most of these scantily clad beauties in towering headdresses were six feet tall, and they were not intellectuals. In fact, they were thick as bricks. Now they were almost piling up on each other, center-stage front, and the show's timing was off.

I hustled backstage and asked the doorman what the hell was going on. He told me an A-list actor was sitting in the front row of the Governor's Box, waving his schlong at them.

"Bullshit!"

"Kid," he said, "it's a perfect match. He's a hell of a swordsman, and those big-titted giraffes are the finest judges of the love muscle in the world."

Our Governor's Box was a small section, festooned, sixth row center, with the best seats in the Amphitheater, reserved for distinguished guests, celebrities from show business, actual governors, and prominent politicians. They were complimentary, of course, but we had never had one of these guests stop the show. Backstage, I sought out Stuttering Sam Dowell, doyenne of the showgirls and daughter of a Fort Worth policeman. Sam assured me, laughing, that the actor had indeed been cantering his limber in plain sight.

My favorite of all the routines in the show was the diving. The featured performers were either Olympic or collegiate champions, except for Stubby Krueger and his professional diving clowns. Jimmy Patterson did a meticulous three-and-a-half front flips every show, and often did four-and-a-half in practice but did not include that one in the act because he could not be positive of his entry into the water.

One afternoon I noticed that an extra clown dive had been added, but it got only a patter of applause. A fully clothed man in a porkpie hat, smoking a pipe, made a mock-stumble off the ten-meter springboard. When I mentioned the mediocre addition backstage after the show, I was told that the newcomer was an unplanned performer. It had been Bing Crosby. The singer had been hoisting a few with Johnny Weissmuller in his dressing room and had decided to get wet with the clowns.

SINCE WE HAD THREE CORPS of girls—pony dancers, swimmers, and showgirls—and I had access to backstage, it was inevitable that I spent considerable time in a tumescent state. The whole idea of theatrical costume designing in revues like ours was to exhibit shapely asses and tilted breasts, and it worked quite well with me. Backstage, my blue uniform merged me into the background, and I was subjected to careless pubic displays as the girls hurried off and on stage.

I had been married less than a year, to a beautiful girl, and was not actually deprived of priapic delights. Still, all those acres of bending, stretching female flesh. . . .

One night, after the last show, I was in the empty Aquacade offices and the phone rang. No higher authority being available, I answered, and an angry doctor insisted I help collect his bills. I slowed him down, because his tirade was purest Bronx, and asked him to go over his complaint again, slowly. He did, and it was graphic.

He was treating seventeen of our performers for various venereal diseases. They were stiffing him for his fees. He did not list the number who were being treated and paying on time. I recognized the names of most of the offending deadbeats. They represented a demographic cross-section of our performers. I promised the doctor I would leave a memorandum on his complaint for the proper party. Thereafter, my voyeurism was less intense.

One afternoon, a show that had begun under bright sunlight darkened as sudden clouds and rain took over. We had been lucky till then, avoiding rain during a performance. As usual, the crowd was seated on the stairways and standing solidly along the ramps. I began coordinating the ushers at the exits so that, if we got thunder and lightning, patrons would not panic trying to leave.

From the comparative dryness of a stairway exit shaft, I listened to the poor bastard doing standup comedy in the rain. I didn't know his name—he wasn't a regular performer—but he never slowed down. He took off his sodden hat and wrung it out and put it back on, shook a fist at the leaking sky, and never stopped doing his shtick. In spite of the lousy acoustics and poor visibility, he worked the huddled crowd patiently.

The titters grew. Laughter spread among the drenched spectators, and he rounded them up like lost sheep, pitching his one-liners at the top ramp as he paced and whirled and cajoled. I laughed involuntarily, wondering why he hadn't been electrocuted by the live mike. He whirled through a big finish and got a huge ovation from the drenched crowd.

Down in the office, after we had emptied the amphitheater, I was told that the surprising performer was a new comic doing a one-shot guest performance. His name was Milton Berle. He had not yet become Uncle Miltie because there were no scheduled television broadcasts. The scientific wonders of the '39 Fair were the tiny demonstration screens, with long lines waiting to see them.

A ROADBLOCK I HAD FEARED proved illusory. With *The Inheritors* finally completed, I asked around and compiled a list of five literary agents. Then, armed with a one-page biography and the manuscript, I went to the Fifth Avenue office of Willis Wing, an affable, big-shouldered man who treated me with courtesy. He said that his client list was full, and he wasn't taking on any more writers. I dropped the bio, the manuscript, and a stamped, self-addressed mailing container on his desk, asked him to read ten pages of it, and left before he could answer. In two weeks, he called the apartment and told Zen he had put the book on the market. A week later, he called and told her Dial Press had agreed to publish. George Joel, the editor there, wanted me to call him.

After its first, tumultuous 1939 season was over, the New York World's Fair closed for the summer. I was not out of a job, however, becoming the night watchman at the shuttered Aquacade Amphitheater. The job was a sinecure. I did nothing from midnight to eight every morning. Since I did not have the necessary license, I couldn't carry a sidearm, but I toured the premises every hour, headquartering in Winkler's control booth, marooned in the sea of seats. The only tough part was getting from the Manhattan apartment to the deserted Flushing fair grounds.

I had observed, just by being on the ground, how business was transacted in New York and its environs. One night, while I was working on my second novel in the control booth surrounded by rows of snow-covered seats, the phone rang and startled me. In that quiet booth, before the dark rows of instrument panels, it had not rung once at that hour.

A harsh voice informed me that four bombs had been planted in the Aquacade. They would go off at two o'clock. The big clock over the panels ticked off seven minutes until two, but when it got to six minutes until two, I wasn't there anymore. I fled all the way to the Fair entrance and waited half an hour in the watchman's shack.

Nothing happened. My precipitous flight, however, was not unwarranted. Rose was paying off everybody to keep his goldmine show going, and there had been violent incidents while the Aquacade was running.

Later, when I switched to working publicity at Rose's nightclub, the Diamond Horseshoe (and it was still publicity then, not public relations), a song-plugger told me that his had been the threatening voice. His wife was a Texas girl, a friend of Zen's, and together they had decided to enliven my lonely vigil at the closed Fair. They had.

The Flushing World's Fair opened its doors for the second year and the world walked in again. Billy Rose's Aquacade got most of the customers. Favorable word-of-mouth from its sensational first year, plus the 99-cent top price, made it available to everyone. Rose put on a duplicate of the show in San Francisco, featuring Weissmuller and competitive swimmer Esther Williams, and another Olympic Gold Medal swimmer, Buster Crabbe, took over the swimming lead in the New York show. In two years, the Aquacade sold fourteen million tickets.

Mike Todd had a revue called "Hot Mikado" at the New York show, but it was a bad second to the Rose show. I met Todd and found him everything Billy was not. Mike was a tough, gregarious showman with great charisma, a blue-sky sharpshooter. Rose remained a somber and aloof personality, but as a professional showman, he was indisputably superior. He would pay any extravagant price for a director or performer he needed, while everybody else involved worked for scale or less.

I was one of the "or less" employees, but the distant Rose always treated me equitably. When the Aquacade closed for good, he moved me into the publicity staff of the Diamond Horseshoe, an opulent rococo production in the basement of the Paramount Hotel, just off Broadway and Times Square. When I moved into

After his stints as a floor manager and nightwatchman for Billy Rose's Aquacade, Phillips was ultimately recruited for his writing talents when hired as a publicist for Rose's magnificent Diamond Horseshoe nightclub and cabaret. Located in the basement of New York's famed Paramount Hotel, the Diamond Horseshoe featured live entertainment from musical acts and comedic plays to dancing revues designed by a young Gene Kelly in his first assignment as a Broadway choreographer. *(New York Public Library - Public Domain)*

the mezzanine office at the hotel, I was in my fourth category of employment by Rose. Outdoor advertising with the red truck, floor manager at two Aquacades, night watchman there, and publicist.

In this last capacity, for a change, I had to use my head.

PUBLIC RELATIONS HAS NOW become a corporate division, but when it was still just publicity there were few women involved. The addition of lingerie to the media-relationship craft has influenced its practice in a number of ways. In 1940, it was simpler. A capable journalist named Mike Mok was my boss, and we churned out stories about Billy Rose's operations and/or plans and tried to palm them off as straight news. Since most Manhattan papers would not touch a dead fish like that, most of these stories went to hinterland papers.

We tried to involve Rose or some of his performers in civic or philanthropic events. Since he was generally disliked by his peers, that usually meant placing performers in positions where their pictures might appear with a Rose credit. Five times a week, we sent interesting paragraphs on New York celebrities to all the daily columnists. The big three were Walter Winchell, Dorothy Kilgallen, and Louis Sobol. Columnist Franklin Pierce Adams, known as FPA, was also opportuned, but his paragraphs had to be more pointed and intellectual, and ours seldom were. There was only one objective: to get Billy Rose's name printed and talked about.

Walter Winchell was then the dominant column power. A brief adverse mention by him could harm or end a show business career. His was the influential voice in the entertainment industry print division. He was a vicious, barely literate ex-hoofer who could reach every producer or nightclub owner who hired entertainment. Kilgallen's column was more sprightly and readable. She was bred in the journalistic tradition, but it still came out fluff. Sobol just strewed recognized names through his work and was more anecdotal.

Richard Maney, the Broadway show representative, was a true genius and madman. He was as apt to skewer his own client as to praise him, and in drunken rages, often did. When I heard of his line, "Women who mix ginger ale and whiskey should be put to the bastinado and reduced to moccasins," I knew there was at least some hope for the street of dreams.

Nearly all of this puffery business consisted of taking in each other's washing, and I was not very good at it. The trade required contacts and I had few. Everything I got was third-hand. I made an effort to join the system but could not fake the bonhomie well.

The show downstairs in the Paramount Hotel basement had a Gay Nineties theme. It worked well in the opulent black-and-scarlet Diamond Horseshoe setting, and the casting, as usual in Billy Rose productions, was meticulous. He hired has-been headliners who still retained some of the magic, and John Murray Anderson's staging was precise.

Eddie Leonard, Gilda Grey, Wini Shaw ("The Lady in Red"), Julian Eltinge, Pat Rooney, and other valorous performers were featured. There was a line of towering showgirls costumed by Raoul Pene DuBois and a pony line trained by former jockey Gene Kelly.

The most interesting part of my work at the nightclub was during the shows, when I sat with journalistic and other media-related guests at the press table. In the afternoons, I wrote releases up in the mezzanine office, but during the two nightly performances, I drank with guests and tried to plant possible stories. Since most of them had been around Broadway far longer than I had, my job also amounted to light pimping. I set up meetings with chorus members for after-the-show celebrations.

Zen had a regular job in the rag district which required her to start work at eight in the morning, but I often made late-night forays into Harlem. My usual goal was a small club on 124th Street that featured a willowy Black vocalist named Jimmy Daniels, who worked without introduction under a single spot and was celebrated for a song called "If You Leave Paris," which often reduced us to drunken tears.

At that time, there was a constant flow of white visitors to Harlem. None of them were harmed, no matter what the hour or their degree of intoxication. The converse was not true. While researching in the main library at 42nd Street, I had met a young Black poet who was in law school and had invited him downtown to have lunch with me. He smiled, shook his head, and said that wasn't such a good idea. In mid-Manhattan, he might or might not get ordered off the premises where we were eating. The year was 1940, and the world was getting ready for a war to save democracy.

In that year, Zen and I had a visitor from the South. It was C., the prematurely white-haired young lawyer I had known in Fort Worth and Longview during my oil-scouting job. He was now practicing in Houston. After checking into the Waldorf-Astoria, he visited us in the apartment and at the show at the Diamond Horseshoe. After that performance was over, we had a final drink at the apartment and he departed, presumably for his hotel.

We had had a luncheon appointment the next afternoon at Lindy's, and when C. did not show up, I walked over to the Waldorf. I called his room from a lobby phone but got no answer. Since C. was an unusually self-reliant type in addition to being a valiant drinker and adroit womanizer, I marked his absence off to one of his usual capers. Still, he was a man who met all his appointments, and it was his first trip to New York, so it worried me.

The next day, his room still did not answer, so I walked over again and enlisted the help of an assistant manager. In his room we found the bed made, and the floor maid reported that it had not been slept in for two days. In his box at the desk, there were several call slips from his Houston law firm but no clue about his whereabouts.

Another day went by with no sign of the Silver Fox. I filed a missing-persons report with the police and called his firm in Houston. None of his partners had heard from him. A detective in a Harlem precinct station said that C. had been in several saloons, had been noticed because of his distinctive thatch of white hair, and had not been feeling any pain. He had been belting away strongly but remained merry and in control. His last reported stop had been in Dickie Wells's Log Cabin, which was not a cathedral of propriety.

I went to Harlem and roamed through some sewer-type establishments, part of the time with a detective but mostly on my own. What I got was an endless mural of agreeable, amused Black faces. None of them led me to C.

On the fifth day after he vanished, I was sitting in my mezzanine office trying to write a speech for dancer Gilda Grey to give on a local radio station about Cracow, Poland, her birthplace, when the phone rang. A brisk voice with a Gullah-African inflection stated that C. was in a cab on his way to the Waldorf. Before I could even say thanks, the line clicked dead.

The Silver Fox was still a trifle crimped when we put him on a plane the next day. But he was in high spirits, said he had recollections of any number of dusky maidens, and had had the finest vacation of his life. When his plane was dwindling south after takeoff, I called his law partner in Houston. "The Fox is now enroute back to you. His plane is nonstop to Atlanta. After that point, he is considered to be in your territory."

MY FIRST NOVEL, *The Inheritors*, was published by Dial Press under the pseudonym Philip Atlee. Previously I had used James Atlee Phillips for my poetry, articles, and short stories, which were beginning to appear in national magazines. There was no specific reason for the change except for the growing premonition that the best possible page in production was entirely blank, unsullied. Until you defaced the virgin page, you faced the possibility of being better than Shakespeare.

Reviews on *The Inheritors* were mixed. A few praised it extravagantly, more saw it as a set of outrageous tirades by a young idealist from the Southwest. The fact that it represented comment from a privileged position was universally remarked, and one well-known lady novelist had some fun with flippant remarks about the author being perforated by all his own merit badges. I appreciated that one because her own work sounded as if it had been scratched out with a sharpened clasp from a garter belt.

Hitler was on the march and, along with many other things, paper became scarce. Dial Press had put out a book by journalist Pierre van Paassen at the same time, and when reprint time came, it properly got the available paper.

Things were different back in Fort Worth. If I could not manage fame in New York or nationally, I managed instant infamy in my hometown. To my delight, sermons were preached against me, and all right-minded people wondered how such an irreproachable mother could produce such a slanderous son. In two Fort Worth bookstores, *The Inheritors* sold out as fast as it was received. For another fifty cents you could buy a list which purportedly supplied the real names of the characters maligned in the novel.

In New York, I achieved the ultimate. The great chronicler of the street of broken dreams, Walter Winchell, gave me a puff in his column. Something like, "Word is going around that Billy Rose has a fledgling Hemingway working in his flack corps."

Heartened by this attention and the high cost of living, in ten days I wrote another novel, *The Case of the Shivering Chorus Girls*. It was no great feat. Recycling all the windy, colorful verbiage I had pounded out in publicity releases, it was a swift and mindless tale of murder at the night club. Midnight winds stirred old newspapers around the statue of Father Duffy guarding Times Square, etc. My role as greeter in the Diamond Horseshoe had been growing erratic because I was drinking too much on the job. I was controlled but kept bumping into people. Once after a memorable binge, I did grab a full page in the *Telegraph* for Rose and his revue headliners, but the day inevitably came when the little showman sent for me. He said flatly that I was getting enough space but was punishing the sauce too hard and my value to him was reduced. In short, I was fired. One of the columnar contributions which had irritated him said: "Billy Rose, the bantam Barnum, is worried about his new Diamond Horseshoe revue. He spent the night pacing around underneath his bed."

I had no complaints. In addition to my disrespect, I was a loose cannon in his accounting. Rose used a system which itemized every pat of butter coming out of the kitchen. Every bottle of spirits from the bar was broken down into individual drinks. Thanks to that system, my largesse in the front of the club couldn't be missed. Zen and I returned to Texas and became part of a nation preparing for war.

It is still possible to read my first novel, which has been out of print for years, but you have to work at it. The Fort Worth Public Library still gets calls for it and will allow their copy to be xeroxed, page-by-page, but only under supervision.

Inspired by Phillips' tenure at Billy Rose's Aquacade, 'The Case of the Shivering Chorus Girls' features the first and only appearance of blind detective Henry Morton Wardlaw, who, following in the Nero Wolfe tradition, solves crimes without ever leaving his penthouse. *(Author Collection)*

PART TWO
THE WAR YEARS

A former WWI military airfield, Hicks was reopened by the United States Army Air Corps in 1940, utilizing civilian flight schools to train thousands of pilots and support personnel needed to fight the war. *(Public Domain)*

MY FIRST PREMONITION THAT THE course of the American government had little to do with the will of the American people came in 1941. Shortly after Zen and I had resettled in Fort Worth, I applied to and was accepted into the Flight Operations Program run by the Gulf Coast Air Corps Training Center. Mere weeks later, and with typical wartime expeditiousness, I found myself twenty-six years old and promoted to Chief Flight Dispatcher at Hicks Field, just outside the Fort Worth suburb of Saginaw. This was a primary training detachment which gave U.S. Army Air Forces (USAAF) military pilots their first sixty hours. American entry into World War Two was being hotly debated, and the Gallup poll showed that eighty percent of the electorate was opposed to our joining the Allies in battle.

The leader of the neutrality forces was Charles Lindbergh, the soft-spoken pilot who had become an internationally famous celebrity because of his solo flight from the US to France. He was seemingly without fault, a modest and intelligent Minnesotan who refused to commercialize his remarkable feat. When he joined

America First, the leading non-interventionist group, President Franklin Roosevelt knew immediately that he was the main obstacle to our joining the European war. The organization was headed by General Robert Wood, Board Chairman of Sears-Roebuck stores.

Roosevelt had a cripple's querulous petulance with anyone who opposed him. He was also so garrulous that insiders said it was difficult to shut him up long enough to consider affairs of state. He was mean, gossipy, and completely ruthless. When he heard that Lindbergh was preparing to make a radio speech opposing our entry into the war, he sent emissaries to the famous pilot, offering to appoint Lindbergh Secretary for Air, a new position in the Cabinet. The speech was given as scheduled. Lindbergh said that three groups were trying to drag the United States into a war against Germany: the British, the bankers, and the Jews.

After that the gloves came off. Lindbergh was vilified by the full force of the Roosevelt administration, and no tactic was too low. The onslaught was led by Harold Ickes, Secretary of the Interior, and was the prototype of the character-assassination tactics perfected much later in the Reagan and Bush campaigns. When Lindbergh asked that his military commission be reactivated, his request was refused. An administration official sent word that if Lucky Lindy, the world's most admired pilot, wished to rejoin the Army Air Corps, he could enlist as an aviation cadet.

On another radio broadcast, shortly before Pearl Harbor, Lindbergh advised his listeners that they would no longer be able to hear his voice. He was correct. The government even blocked his attempts to join Pan American Airways as a civilian pilot.

I did not, of course, know about these inside particulars at the time. But even from a prairie flying field in Texas, I could recognize the hatchet job being done on an authentic hero.

I HAVE SEEN FEW ASTONISHING things in my life. Among them are the Panama Canal, the Himalayas, and the Taj Mahal by moonlight. Although it took me awhile to perceive it, the way my government mounted and refined a pilot-training program ranks near the top. After becoming chief dispatcher at Hicks Field, north of Fort Worth, I was at an ideal observation post.

Before 1940, the US was training about five hundred military pilots a year. General Hap Arnold of the Army Air Forces, a remarkable unsung hero of World War Two, saw our predicament clearly and selected nine civilian flight-training contractors. He paid them handsomely to start a huge military training program in a country which was resolutely opposed to entering the European war. In scattered locations, they gave selected cadet candidates their first sixty hours of pilot training.

At Hicks Field, one of those primary training detachments, we had 125 aircrafts, consisting of Stearman biplanes and Fairchild low-wing monoplanes. There were four thousand cadets in each class, and it was my job to see that planes stayed off the ground most of the time. The contractors were paid by hours flown. The instructors were all civilian, and if they cleared our course, the cadets went on to basic and advanced military training. In less than three years the country produced the largest corps of military pilots in history.

The training was not difficult at first because we got the eager beavers, boys who could already fly or who had begun flight training. Some of our candidates were already officers, coming straight from West Point graduation. Others were country boys who had remarkable hand-eye coordination from hunting and fishing. Our sixty hours of training were rigorous, with a high washout rate, but it beat hell out of marching as a grunt.

There were tragedies. One cadet from Venezuela, the son of a high government official there, was facing elimination because he consistently over-controlled. Prior to his final check ride, he told his barrack mates that he had no intention of going home a failure. He didn't. After the check ride, while their plane was preparing to land, he wrestled control away from his instructor, and they both died as he slammed on full power and plunged into the ground.

Keeping scores of light planes aloft for precise periods required total concentration. Our best at it was a bulky Oklahoman named Clarence. In the few lulls, he helped us all relax with anecdotes of his home in the Indian Nations section of the Sooner state. He said that his fondest memory was camping out with nothing between him and the cold ground but a thin little Indian girl. He told us that he had once taken time off from tending his moonshine still to take a crap in deep woods, but when he attempted to rise he felt terrible shooting pains. He was in dreadful agony for an hour, unable to stand up. "Problem was," he told us, "my boot heels were pinning my balls to the ground."

The duty hours at the airfield were rigorous but the living was easy. Zen and I had a comfortable cottage leased and a Pontiac convertible, both gifts from her doctor father, and on weekends, we used his cabin cruiser on Lake Worth. Its ice chests and bar were kept well stocked, and we never lacked for attendant lords and ladies. Hitler had bludgeoned Poland and was poised to take the Ruhr. Draft cards were showing up in almost every mailbox, and a few protesters were taking off for Canada or Sweden. I could afford to be complacent because my employment status was securely exempted. Some candidates contrived to show blood in the urine and others took on swishes and announced they were homosexual. Sometimes it worked, and I wondered if R. in California was being called up.

On one of our nocturnal lake cruises, a well-upholstered heir to a large oil fortune got smashed and announced that I was lucky I had not characterized him in my shilling-shocker book. I soothed

Buster by telling him that I had considered using him but after checking into his background had concluded that he would not warrant a paragraph. Insulted, he demanded to be returned to the dock, and we complied at flank speed.

In 1942, Zen announced that she was pregnant, and that caused me to iris in suddenly on our relationship. My young wife was the tall, vibrant, model-type, a green-eyed beauty, but she had a problem. It was called Raynaud's syndrome, an affliction of unknown cause which affects the upper extremities from a circulatory standpoint. It was linked with Buerger's disease, which usually occurs in the lower male extremities. In both, the condition can worsen enough to cause amputations.

Zen had long been using Nembutal, and her lingerie drawer was filled with tougher items like Percodan, Demerol, and painkillers I had never heard of. Her father was a pillar of medical integrity except where she was concerned, and she could virtually write her own prescriptions.

As she thickened, we tried to follow all the prenatal rules. Her drinking and medication were severely restricted. In 1943, our son Shawn was born with no problems. He was a blond cherub, vocal and boisterous.

BY 1943, THE ENTIRE STATE OF TEXAS seemed an armed camp. Fort Worth had a bomber factory and an Army Air Force base in addition to the primary flight-training detachment where I worked. The bars, airports, and train stations were sluicing young men around constantly, and each of the state's 254 counties seemed to hold some kind of military facility.

Old rules of propriety had relaxed, and every red-blooded American could curse the Boche or Nip and have another drink. Girls who hadn't, did; it seemed a part of the national fever. A little loin music for victory. Our cabin-cruiser parties became more riotous. The guest lists included foreigners taking flight training, bomber plant officials, and boys with shipping orders to places they had never heard of before.

My older brother, Eddie the lawyer, was in the Signal Corps. He would endure New Guinea, and end the war with the Judge Advocate's staff in Tokyo. Ollie-katz, the brother just below me, was an amiable giant, also a lawyer, and had been the only real patriot in the family, having enlisted in the Texas National Guard in 1939, long before Pearl Harbor. Supposedly in the artillery, he had become frustrated by having wooden sticks represent rifles and dump trucks represent tanks. Turning to boxing, he took out his anger on sparring partners and punched his way to the heavyweight championship of the 36th Division.

When he fought in the national Golden Gloves finals, I flew to Chicago and checked into the Palmer House. One of the night clerks there was a fight fan, and since Olcott and I had the same first name and were both from Fort Worth, he concluded that I was the combatant. For two nights in a row, Ollie-katz had knockouts, and I showed up at the hotel plastered to the gills. The night clerk asked me how I could lush it up so thoroughly and still win. I assured him that it posed no problem.

The night of the heavyweight finals, Olcott was up against a

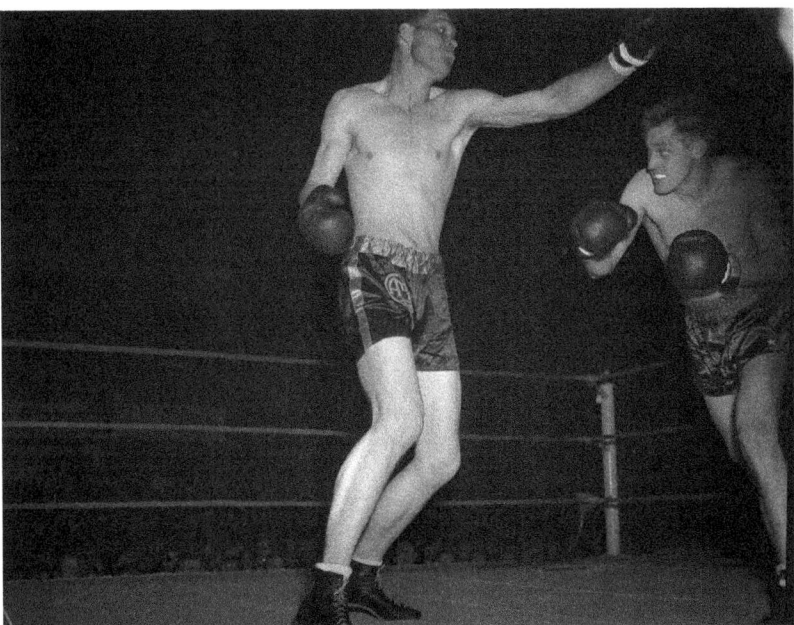

The tallest Phillips brother fought his way to clinch the Heavyweight Championship of the Texas National Guard 36th Division, then went on to a winning performance in the Golden Gloves finals, ultimately losing by decision. *(Author Collection)*

Black fighter named Hubert Hood, a rough puncher. While the introductions were being made, a nice Chicago lady sitting in the same row leaned across her husband and asked me about my feelings. What was the Southern attitude toward mixing the races in fistic combat? In my best liberal stance, I assured her that my friends were only interested in seeing the best man win.

The bell rang. Hubert Hood shuffled smoothly across the ring and tagged my brother with a straight right hand, so hard that his knees buckled. I stood up, trembling with rage, and shouted, "Kill that Black sonavabitch!" As I sat down, the nice Chicago lady was regarding me with loathing. Ollie-katz came on strong as usual and won the third round but lost the decision.

The publicity got him sent to Officer Candidate School. A former honor student at Rice, he finished the war on Okinawa, in charge of the garbage detail. The youngest Phillips brother, David, had been a fledgling actor and toured in a road company of a Broadway hit. He took gunnery training in Brownsville and was assigned to a B-24 turret. His bomber was knocked out of the sky over Vienna on a raid from Palermo. He parachuted from the burning plane, was captured by the Germans, and spent a year in a stalag. Later, he would become a ranking CIA officer for covert operations in the Western hemisphere.

Two years after the Japanese attack, I remained the only civilian of the four brothers, because my flight-training work was a splendid draft board dodge. That hectic summer saw one Fort Worth celebrator take his Chris-Craft speedboat far out into the lake, wind it up to the red line, and see how far he could beach it. Another local madman concluded a spat with his wife by trying to fly a Cub into her bedroom window. He nearly made it. The wings came off, but he got most of the fuselage inside.

And along came Owen Johnson. He was a personable Pan Am vice president who was covering the country, recruiting pilot and flight operations personnel for the Chinese national airline. The company was styled China National Aviation Corporation, CNAC, and was forty-nine percent owned by Pan American Airways and fifty-one percent by Chiang Kai-Shek's Kuomintang government in Chungking. It had been set up to fly personnel and freight across the Himalayas to China, all other sea and land routes having been blocked by the Japanese.

I was beginning to tire of the constant concentration demanded by flight training at Hicks Field. Every six weeks, we got another class of four thousand cadets, and there was a lot of backbiting and politicking in the civilian training cadre. When the Pan Am veep came on one of our midnight boating trips, I watched him proselytizing

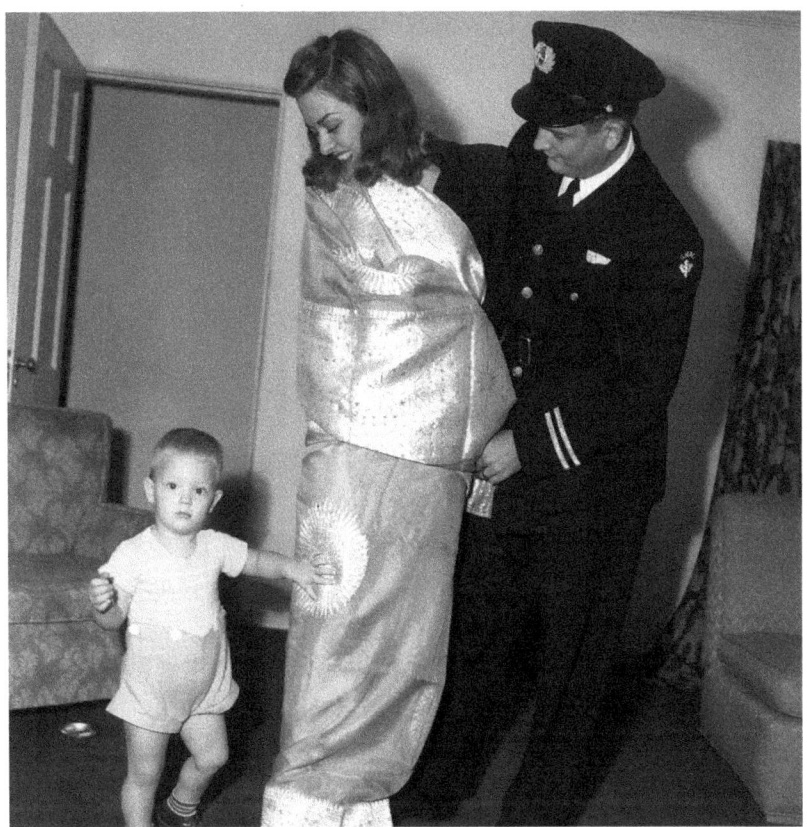

Shown left to right: Shawn Phillips, Joyce Phillips (née Clayton), and James Atlee Phillips. The author parlayed his airfield training at Hicks Field in Ft. Worth into a job as Chief of Flight Operations for China National Aviation Corporation (CNAC), where he managed thousands of resupply flights over the Himalayan 'Hump' from Dinjan, India to Chinese and American military forces in Kunming, China. *(UTA Archives)*

among the merry celebrants. Principally, he was wooing pilot instructors with multi-engine time. Almost as an afterthought, he emerged from the cabin bar with another drink and asked if I would be interested in working operations in the China-Burma-India theater.

"No," I said. "I'm not interested. I'm ready to sign a contract."

Three weeks later, I was at the Floridian Hotel in Miami Beach, waiting to be called for a military flight halfway around the world.

MIAMI WAS ONE OF THE MAJOR departure centers for the Air Transport Command. From it, international flights went to all US military sectors, and passengers were emplaned on a strict priority system. I never knew a Priority One and suspected that that category was limited to the President, his Chief of Staff, and the Shroud of Turin. Generals, bird colonels, admirals, and commodores were Two's, and civilians like me barely qualified for Three because we were employed by an airline flying through a combat area.

We were dispatched on a space-available basis. For that reason, once we checked into the Floridian Hotel, we could not leave its grounds until we were called for flight. Since our little group wore civilian clothes and carried only blind orders to depart the States, we were regarded as somewhere between spies and draft dodgers.

Waiting to be called, and packed for it, we lounged on the hotel's beach and in its bar. My first night there I bought a drink for an ATC co-pilot who worked on the Far East run. He outlined the route they flew to India: Miami to Rancho Boyeros [now José Marti] airport outside Havana, then Port of Spain in Trinidad, then Belem and Natal, Brazil. The long Atlantic Ocean jump to Ascension Island was next, followed by Accra, Maiduguri, and Khartoum in Africa. Al Masirah Island, Karachi, and Calcutta took the C-54 to the end of the outward trip.

By a method not yet known to me, my mother had inveigled my brothers and me into browsing through encyclopedias and everything else in our large library. Somewhere in my visual travels, I had come upon the reflection that there were limitless universes in a single raindrop. Beginning with that, I had evolved the singular concept that everything in my life was unreal, that everything I saw was an illusion, sets being thrown up suddenly before my appearance, and struck as quickly when I had passed by.

This conceit represented such an enormous job of stage management, whole worlds being swept away as I passed, to be replaced by newly created ones, that I seemed to be on a pointless passage. Hannibal and the elephants, Tamerlane and his yurts, Lincoln swinging his axe . . . Waiting to be called in the Floridian, I smiled at my own egomania, because it would soon be tested. Our flight path to China passed over the Taj Mahal. I meditated on the anonymous scene-shifter getting that one ready.

We were not called for two days. At noon on the third day, I went down to the hotel's strip of beach and loosened up with a crawl stroke beyond the slight surf. As I came wading out of the water and picked up my towel, I heard an excited voice. It was coming from a portable radio next to a pot-bellied character lounging on the sand with his wife and two small children.

There was a roaring crowd noise behind the excited announcer's voice. The 1943 World Series was on the air, Yankees against St. Louis. I stood about eight feet away from the little family, toweling myself and hoping to catch the score.

The owner of the radio had been sprawled with his head on his hairy forearms. When my shadow fell across him, he turned his head, saw me, reached out and turned off the radio. The announcer went mute in mid-shout.

I stared down at the lounging man in disbelief, thinking he was the meanest-minded sonofabitch I had ever encountered. As I walked back through the hotel garden, I met my ATC co-pilot friend, hustling toward the parking lot. He was in uniform and carried his map case.

"You're booked," he shouted. "Catch the four o'clock bus."

I nodded and waved. The summons had finally come. As I walked into the men's room on the ground floor of the hotel and urinated into one of the white marble troughs, my pulse was quickening.

On the wall above the urinal was a bold scrawl:

PEARL HARBOR, HELL! CALL PEARL JOHNSON 422 5178

The scrawl was a grace note and made the global war believable, banishing the sorry bastard with the radio.

Pearl Johnson was worth fighting for.

YOUNG MEN DO NOT GO TO WAR to follow the flag or support just causes. They go to get out of the house. To escape the tedium of Mom's apple pie, the baby's howling. Ostensibly, they are going to fight and become heroes, but the fact is that they have had a look at the compartmented future looming ahead. That drab destiny was to be avoided at all costs, even if it meant slaughtering strangers.

My flight to the war in China was interesting. Want a fresh pineapple? A beach boy in Natal will slice the top off one with his cutlass. Want a drink in tropic weather? Pure lime juice, from fruit not long off the tree, poured over shaved ice and mixed with powdered sugar. En route to Karachi, I touched four continents.

I finally saw the Taj Mahal and was thunderstruck. I proved my earlier contention that the entire universe was fake, assembled to meet me as I approached and torn down after I passed. The Taj, when I approached it in a plane, had its spires covered by scaffolding. Later I was told that it was being cleaned, but the truth is that whoever was assembling these fake universes had flopped. They had been caught building it as I approached.

My job was satisfactory. On clear days, from my office in the foothills of the Himalayas, Mt. Everest could be seen, with snow flags pluming off its crest. Around our small airport in upper Assam, the jump-off point for the Hump flight, were miles of premium tea bushes. The long green valley was framed by groves of flame-of-the-forest trees, with mighty mountain ramparts barring the way to China.

Dinjan was the name of our station. Within a few miles of its runway were our two hostels for flight and maintenance personnel and a radio station which worked for our base in Calcutta to the capital of China, Chungking. From that river sanctuary, the thoroughly corrupt Kuomintang government accepted the US lend-lease largesse we flew across the peaks.

My job was to handle flight operations in Dinjan, scheduling all flights to China. I assigned the planes and flight crews and coordinated the maintenance on a fleet bigger than American Airlines. The difference was that we were a civilian operation flying over combat terrain. Because of our hazardous routes, we went to a lot of funerals.

My immediate superior in the Assamese jump-off airport for the Hump flight was a stocky man with a taciturn manner named Hugh Woods. Originally from Kansas, he was an authentic China hand, an old-line pilot, and I nearly made a bad mistake in dealing with his reticence. In outlining my duties, Woods stressed that my previous experience had been in scheduling flight cadets for set periods over safe terrain. With CNAC, the operations were diametrically opposed. First, no pilot ever had to accept a scheduled flight. The option was written into his contract. He did not even have to give a reason. Secondly, our flights round-tripped the most dangerous route in the world, both in terrain and weather.

We were using DC-3s, and unless you flew the far south routes, which were controlled by Japanese airports, the flight to Kunming often tested the plane's service ceiling. Severe icing of the carburetors, wings, and props occurred. Winds aloft of unbelievable force might be encountered over the peaks. Many of our loads were hazardous. We carried munitions, explosives, and chemical weapons.

In his briefing, Captain Woods said matter-of-factly that a major part of our airline's activity involved smuggling, mostly gold but also a constant stream of Swiss, English, and American currency. Penicillin tablets were worth $1.25 apiece on the China side. A standard .45 caliber pistol you could buy for thirty dollars in Miami was worth two hundred in Kunming. A gold-plated Parker fountain pen was worth fifty bucks. These inflated values were based on the fact that all traffic to China except for our air route was blocked by the Japanese.

The flight personnel I would be assigning consisted of a rotating pool of 103 white European captains, three Chinese captains, Chinese copilots and radio operators, and an influx of white copilots from the States who would be flown in the right cockpit seat, until they either got killed or qualified as captains. On the line, we had over fifty Chinese mechanics supervised by a handful of European chiefs.

All the Chinese personnel except for the few captains were housed in a hostel in the Balijan district, and Europeans were housed in another, larger lodge, framed by immaculate rows of tea bushes. There were several herds of wild elephants roaming the Assam valley, but they rarely posed an airport problem except for the radio station. They sometimes scratched against and knocked down bamboo poles carrying telephone lines to the operations office from the field.

Finally, said Woods, in the matter of personal hygiene I must be careful of the slit trenches which surrounded our airstrip. In case of Japanese air raids, the natural tendency was to dive into one of the trenches. That would be a mistake. They were filled with "coolie" shit, he said.

Having brought me up to date, Woods got in his little Vauxhall sedan and drove off to his bungalow, several miles from Dinjan. I wandered down the flight line to the maintenance area. Art Prendergast, an oil-smeared gnome, was supervising several plug changes, scrambling around on the pipe scaffolding. When I offered him a drink of warm gin, he came scrambling down.

Art wasn't sure he was going to tolerate me. He was known as a fiend for work, an extemporizing chief of mechanics who had seen a good many of the hotshots recruited by Pan Am go sour on the Hump. They mostly schemed to get back to the Royal Calcutta golf course and the whorish delights of that city's Kariah Road. As he took his second belt from the gin bottle I said that Hugh Woods had filled me in but that he seemed remote and low-key. Art took a piece of clean cloth from his back coverall pocket and mopped at his sweaty face.

"If you intend to hang around here long, Phillips," he said, "it might be a good idea to get your head out of your ass. Three years ago Captain Woods took off from Hong Kong for Chungking with twenty-one passengers. A squadron of Zeroes forced him down in the Pearl River. While he and the passengers were swimming to shore, the Nip pursuits came down on the deck, strafed and machine-gunned them in the water. Only Woods and four passengers made it to the shore."

STRANDED BY THE VAGARIES of a global war in a remote corner of the world, I had a serious problem. It was part morality, part pride, and involved self-definition. My job in the CBI theater was minor but directly involved the functioning of a vital supply route. Chiang Kai-Shek and his Kuomintang government in Chungking were entirely corrupt. Everything they did was aimed at influencing the increased flow of American aid for their own enrichment.

They were not China, however. That country had produced rich cultures when my own forebears were still living in trees. The men I worked with were mercenaries from all over the Western world. They, too, had come to loot a buck from the Japanese dislocation of Asian borders.

I decided to play it straight down the middle. The planes were there to fly supplies over the big rock-candy mountains. The need for what they could furnish was obvious. My motivation was also obvious: to fly the planes as efficiently and as often as possible without fretting about vitiating sideshows like smuggling and Chinese politics. Or, even by remote extension, the American cripple who was president or the doughty old drunk who was prime minister. And the first requirement in my niche was that I would be like Caesar's wife in every detail.

The pilots trooped past my office to their planes at all hours, bulky and irritable in leather gear, juggling map cases and parachutes. Gradually they turned into people, with crotchets and wry humors. Charley Sunby, round-shouldered and mostly silent, was a Russian said to have thirty thousand hours in his logs. He returned from hair-raising weather or sunny skies with the same comment: "It's all right." On a day when we lost four planes, crashed and burned on the Suifu hills, Sunby turned up late. He said that it had been all right.

Before every trip, the pilots were handed mimeographed weather reports, gathered within the last two hours from meteorological stations scattered across the Himalayas. Catfish Raines, from Nevada, always crumpled his up and threw it away without even glancing at it. When I asked him why, the tall pilot shrugged. "I don't give a fuck what the weather is," he said. "I'm going anyway, ain't I?"

He had me there.

My own favorite was a blustering, sneezing man who was laughing his way through the war. He had flown everywhere, from South America's Gran Chaco to being private pilot for film actress Ann Harding. His asthma was almost killing him and he gleefully predicted his own early demise. Once, he got reciprocating bearings from the Kunming tower, ran out of gas, and had to bail out over unmapped terrain. Four days later, he walked out of the mountains, rejoined us in the Dinjan hostel, and said it was my fault. I knew his asthma was bad the day he vanished but had sent him anyway.

Jimmy Scoff had a cherubic face under a balding pate. I inveigled him into doing a second round trip across the Hump one day by promising all the vanilla ice cream he could eat, with chocolate sauce on it. Such dessert was rare because supplies had to be flown into our station from Calcutta, and space was at a premium. Jimmy came back from his second trip beaming and I personally drove him to the pilots' hostel.

White-robed bearers were lined up in the dining room, regal in turbans. Scoff sat at the high table, banging his spoon in anticipation as a platter of five white mounds was set before him and the head bearer poured hot chocolate sauce over them. Beaming, Jimmy took a spoonful.

His jaw action slowed in disbelief. Grabbing the platter, he hurled it across the dining room at me, cursing in several languages including Swahili. The chocolate sauce was real, but the white mounds weren't ice cream but artfully sculptured cold mashed potatoes.

Eighteen of our pilots had joined the China airline after Chennault's Flying Tigers mercenary group had been disbanded. Some of the Tigers had joined the newly formed 14th Air Force but the ones we got were rough as cobs, like Bob Prescott, a hard driver who found any disaster hilarious. After the war, he helped found and was president of the Flying Tiger freight airline, a huge success which was itself acquired by Federal Express in 1988.

A pilot I watched with particular interest was Roy Farrell of Vernon, Texas. He was a bustling, voluble man, the object of regard by our Chinese mechanics. They kept a running line on all our pilot candidates and Loy Fal, which was as close as they could come to Farrell's name, was their choice to buy the farm quickest. It had come to their attention that he had never flown anything larger than a Cub before he arrived on the Hump.

Loy Fal, undaunted, exasperated several check pilots and evolved as one of the best over the big mountains. He later flew his own DC-3 from the States to Shanghai and founded or co-founded three airlines: Amphibian, Macao, and Cathay Pacific, which remains the dominant Orient-based line.

We had only a few Chinese captains. I never understood whether it was because of insufficient training or concentration, but many Chinese could fly co-pilot for several years but flunk out as captains. While undergoing final checks, they would do almost everything perfectly but fail to lower the gear when landing.

An outstanding exception was George Huang. He came from a rich Chinese family, never seemed to be serious, and never missed a turn. He had been educated in Europe and was half-Scottish, a mixture which produces handsome issue.

Most pilots wanted this plane or that one for various reasons. Some wouldn't accept a plane with a malfunctioning heater. "Gentleman George" Huang never made any such requests. Bundled to the ears and laughing like a child, he accepted what he was assigned, flew the Hump in all weathers and, if asked, flew another round trip the same day.

Between trips, while his plane was being unloaded, loaded, and serviced, Huang lounged in my office and asked questions about the United States. I was glad to serve as his teacher. I told him that all funds resulting from Post Office stamp sales went directly and tax-free to a Connecticut family named Tuttle. This was because of distinguished service by the original Seth Tuttle to the fledgling American Revolution. The award had been instigated by Benjamin Franklin at the Continental Congress, was part of the Constitution, and extended into perpetuity.

"God Almighty," said awed George Huang. "How much have they made off it so far?"

The handsome pilot would wander off to his plane and make another mountain crossing, either the Kunming, the Chungking, or the Suifu. He discussed the Seth Tuttle legacy with other pilots. Inevitably they told him I was a lying bastard, and he would come charging across the Dinjan runway to face me again. I deflected his laughing protests by saying that if he didn't want true American history, just forget it.

Often, I felt more like a nanny than an operations officer. At three in the morning, I would mount the stairs to the long barracks room filled with rows of translucent cubicles, the mosquito-netted beds where sleeping pilots lay. Flashlight in one hand and chart in the other, I would go down the aisles shaking assigned pilots awake. Some came awake hard. Robbie Robertson, of Georgia, had a checkered past, and always had his hand on the .44 pistol under his pillow.

When those headed for the flight line were awake, I went downstairs to check the dining room, where the turban-clad waiters were putting breakfast on the table. The line of jeeps and command cars was formed up under the veranda. Half an hour earlier, another small fleet had picked up the co-pilots and radio operators at the Chinese hostel. At the field, I sat behind my desk with the tower and weather receivers growling behind me and the teletype clicking and pinging. I handed out freshly inked reports of conditions on the mountains, counting in my head as the planes cranked up in their dark revetments.

One by one, they requested the tower, in irritated jargon, for taxi permission. After checking out their magnetos, they came rolling in muted thunder under my office window, requesting permission to take off and lift out of the Assam valley of the upper Brahmaputra toward the jagged ramparts of the Himalayas.

The mounting planes would pass over herds of elephants. Originally, the great beasts had trumpeted and scattered in confusion, but as our flights increased they stood motionless, their ears fanning.

To truly appreciate a war, you must have an enemy active in the neighborhood. We had one. The Japanese had two divisions in upper Burma and held most of that country from Rangoon northward. Merrill's Marauders were below us in the jungle but were gradually being worn down by attrition, and we had not yet taken Myitkyina. Vinegar Joe Stilwell was trying to make the Chinese fight, but it was an uphill battle. Chiang didn't want them fighting. He might lose some of them.

The Japanese air force had bases less than a half hour's flight from our Dinjan strip. My third day on duty at the field, I heard an approaching, unsynchronized humming and noticed laborers running off the field. That was unusual because these laborers usually just plodded along with their burdens. The pilots had told me that Nip bombers in groups usually sounded out of sync. I bolted out of the office toward my jeep, being joined by Art Prendergast and several of his mechanics. Covered by hangers-on, the jeep went careening off the field and down the dusty road. The uneven, massed humming increased behind us.

From the safety of a bamboo grove, we watched as enemy bombers passed over Dinjan at twenty thousand feet. Zero pursuit planes were flying top cover. The sun was shining brightly. The falling sticks of bombs bracketed the intersection of the runway, throwing up clods of dirt and asphalt. It was precision bombing. They didn't tear up much because there wasn't much to tear up. The worst damage was to several rows of tea bushes north of the runway.

After the bombers had made two runs, over and back, they returned to Burma. The Zeroes came down and strafed the dirt roads, killing a few water buffalo but missing our long office shed and maintenance scaffolding. Before their sounds of departure had died away completely, waves of local airport workers were swarming over the Dinjan runway intersection, patching up the negligible damage there.

FOR A YEAR, MY SERVICE in the Assam station unreeled in a kaleidoscopic blur of endless trips between the pilots' hostel and Dinjan strip. I often worked around the clock, assigning, transporting, and greeting crews in a monomania of trips recorded. Each pilot was under contract and was paid on the basis of hours flown. After sixty hours, they went on golden time at a higher hourly fee.

To accentuate our ever-increasing number of round trips, I put colored charts on the office walls. Every pilot could glance at it and tell how his efforts were mounting or, as with a few laggards, how they were comparing with the leaders. One day, one of the junior captains taxied by my office and came walking back without his plane, chute banging his ass, to report that he had hit a railroad train on a small narrow-gauge line at the edge of the field. Another first.

My sleep was brief, desultory, and filled with crashing aircraft. Often enough, while awake, we had to send body bags up the peaks to retrieve victims. Alone in the jeep one night, returning to the pilots' hostel, I rounded a turn and confronted a tiger crossing the road. Since he had the right of way, I stopped quickly. His orange eyes were blazing as I switched off the lights. He smelled rank. I could hear his throttled growling as he continued across the road.

I was only an operations clerk in the airline's hierarchy but an indispensable link to its mounting flight success. My goal was simple. I never let an operational aircraft sit idly on the ground. The pilots had a contractual right to refuse any flight. They didn't have to give any reason. When they refused—and very few of them did—I just moved on, seeking another volunteer.

It wasn't the Japanese who finally slowed me down but a sebaceous cyst on the scrotum. It was a painless tumor, but rockets went off in my head. In my ceaseless trips to the airport I had often seen natives being trundled along in homemade carts, supine because they had basketball-sized testicles. Assam was filariasis country. Woody, my boss, had explained that several uncut wooded tracts around the huge tea gardens incubated anopheles and mansonia mosquitoes, which vectored microfilariae. The planters of Assam had isolated these wooded patches where the mosquitoes bred in order to restrict their spreading. It seemed to work. Most of the natives were immune to the threat. We had mosquito nets. And I had a swelling scrotum.

A Hindu doctor from Chabua was sent for. His name was Mukerji, and he hated white men and had always wanted to cut on one. He took a blood sample, vanished, and came back three days later. He put me on my back, swabbed my privates with an orange lotion and lanced the cyst. It released a foul-smelling exudate which stained the mosquito netting with the force of its discharge. When I showed him the penicillin tablets we had brought up from Calcutta, he nodded, told me how to take them, and vanished again.

BECAUSE THE DOCTOR HAD INSTRUCTED me to stay in bed several days, Captain Woods made an arrangement for me to move into the large Proudfoot bungalow. This was the home of the tea plantation owner on whose grounds our Balijan airstrip had been built. The Proudfoot family was Scottish and lived in almost baronial simplicity. The house swarmed with native bearers. The thinking was that I could recuperate there unvexed by all-night poker games, constant turmoil, and the lethal bamboo juice available in the airline's hostel.

Life in the guest bedroom at the Proudfoot place was peaceful. My God, it was peaceful! Chimes for dinner, rung by barefoot servants. Meals on the dot, everything immaculate, even to the starched white napkins artfully folded in the shape of swans. I lay in bed, read tattered Penguin paperbacks, listened to the constant run-ups on plane engines and the thunder of their takeoffs for China. But three days was enough. I went back to work, though I continued to bunk there.

Four days after I had returned to the firing line, I miscalculated the dosage of Dikum Death during a poker game at the hostel. Dikum Death was named after its place of origin. The native bootleggers who made it would obligingly stick on any label you liked. Whiskey, brandy, wine, it all came out of the same vat. When the poker game broke up, about four a.m., I drove the command car I was using straight home, to the Proudfoot bungalow. By straight I mean avoiding the lanes, cutting through the carefully tended rows of tea bushes. Since the command car weighed nearly as much as a tank, it cleared a path right up to the bungalow doors.

At noon that day, Proudfoot called Captain Woods and said that since I seemed fully recovered, it might be time for me to move back to the pilots' hostel. This transfer was made with dispatch, and I got an insight into the tea business. After an assessment of the damage, I was made to pay for several rows of uprooted plants at five dollars a bush.

EVEN THOUGH THE U.S. AIR FORCE had cranked up its own Himalayan supply route near us, at Chabua, the fate of our section of the CBI theater of war seemed ominous. Not long before, one of our pilots had blown far past us, west of the Brahmaputra River, when returning from China. He made a miraculous moonlit landing athwart a small stream. We got him out by landing nearby at a new airstrip called Sohrbog, one of a series of emergency fallback fields being built across the top of India. Sohrbog had no people on it, only a hastily built facility in the wilderness.

The two Imperial Japanese divisions in North Burma had attacked Imphal and Dimapur. They were trying to break into India below us and were being repelled in fierce combat by British troops trying to keep them out of Manipur province. Rommel was mopping up in the North African desert, and it appeared possible that he might go all the way to Suez. If he did, and the Japanese could strike across India to Karachi, the Axis forces might cut us off entirely. Everything we got was airlifted from Calcutta or slow-freighted up the Brahmaputra River. Evacuation orders had been cut for all military and civilian personnel in the Assam valley. A contingency escape route was worked out across the mountains to China.

I was in my office one afternoon, bringing the flight maps on the wall up to date, when a tall, dark-haired American mechanic named Hal Hughes wandered in. I glanced over my shoulder at him. He was a recent arrival. I had seen him at the hostel but didn't know him well. "Something for you," he said, and dropped a square of cardboard on my desk. I nodded and he went back toward the maintenance shed.

What he had left was a foot-square cartoon, done with a highly professional line. It depicted a background of towering storming peaks, with lightning arrowing off them. There was one central figure leaning on an oversized bludgeon bigger than a baseball bat.

The figure was uniformed, sleeves rolled up, with the CNAC insignia on the battered flight cap. Over the pocket was a badge which read JYP LEGREE. Dark glasses and a cat-o-nine-tails dangled from the belt. My right foot was on the neck of a battered, supine pilot, and three bloodhounds were sniffing at him. Back of this scene, in the foothills, were three more pilots skulking next to a heat-fatigued and collapsing C-47 plane. And in a balloon streaming from the mouth of Legree was the following legend:

The boys don't need but little persuadin'.
They'd rather fly than eat—Just tell 'em
Which plane to take and away they go—

Looking the drawing over, I smiled, because it represented a prevailing point of view. Mostly, I was astonished by its composition and professional execution. I meant to walk down to thank Hughes for it, but the teletype clicked out trouble and I was diverted to something else.

I thought of it again a few days later but was told that Hughes was in Calcutta helping check a new plane from the States. The plane took off from Dum Dum Airport the next afternoon with eleven people on board including Hal Hughes and, on the flight to join us in Dinjan, encountered heavy turbulence. It was blown over us in the night into Tibet. So far as I know, the wreckage was never located.

Hal, I regret I never knew you. But your fine and funny cartoon still hangs upon my wall.

THE MONTHS RAN ALONG in merging lockstep days. After savage fighting in Manipur, British forces repelled the Japanese and began a drive to recapture Rangoon. Orde Wingate, that strange tactical genius, died in a plane crash, and Vinegar Joe Stilwell besieged Myitkyina, the key to North Burma. Joe was an original. Given command of Chinese troops, he lived among them like a company commander and turned them into a fighting force for the first time. To him, the corrupt and enigmatic Chiang was known as Peanut. When Lord Mountbatten visited him in the field, Stilwell told him that His Lordship had more planes in his personal escort than Vinegar Joe had in his air force.

There came a day when the CNAC flight line was shut down because all available petrol had been switched to Stilwell's forces. The sight of all our grounded motionless transports galled me. By a remarkable display of stupidity, over a hundred thousand gallons of aviation gas, in drums, had been lost on a short railway line between the Brahmaputra River and our field. We trucked it in and began to filter it with chamois skins, a hot and arduous process. I pursued it around the clock, however, raging at laggards, and we began to hand-funnel it into the planes.

George Huang was assigned the test plane. I sat exhausted in my office and listened to him running up the engines. No call for taxi or takeoff permission followed, and both motors were shut down. George reappeared in my office and asked me to drive him back to the plane. When we got there, he was still unsmiling. Under the wing, he opened the sump drain from the main tank and invited me to test it with my fingers. "This fuel isn't safe," he said. "I won't fly the plane."

I nodded. He was driven back to the hostel, and I had the tanks drained and the petrol filtered again. After another forty-eight hours, Bob Prescott flew the plane to Kunming without incident, and we slowly got the fleet in the air again.

A week later, I drove out to Woods's bungalow and informed him that my usefulness to the China line was ended. The pilots felt, perhaps rightfully, that I had tried to send them at the mountains with unsafe fuel. He asked if I wanted to go back to the States, and I said yes.

I requested ship passage back if possible, explaining that the draft board would be awaiting me with a 1A, and a sea voyage would give me a breather. Woods smiled at that and reminded me that both the Indian and Pacific Oceans were 100 percent danger waters for mariners.

Three weeks later, I started down the Hooghly River from Calcutta on the *Cape Lambert*, a C-type freighter, as the only passenger. The ship would make Colombo, Ceylon, then down through the Indian Ocean and under Australia, then pass through the Bass Strait into the Pacific, making Hilo, Hawaii, on the way to San Francisco.

THE LONG VOYAGE HOME, from halfway around the world through dangerous waters in a blacked-out freighter, took three weeks. In the port of Colombo, the *Cape Lambert* anchored in the roadstead at midnight. Watching from a wing of the darkened bridge, I saw a launch speed out of the dock area and stand off the freighter. There was a raucous blare across the intervening water as the port captain addressed us through his hand-held hailer-horn. "What is the name of your vessel, where is she bound, and what are her requirements in the Port of Colombo?"

A few feet away from me, on our bridge perch high over the tossing launch, Captain Albert Herre answered the hailer on his own horn, saying that we were the S.S. *Cape Lambert*, home port San Francisco, California, and that we would require water, marine oil, and food supplies. We were ordered to tie up at Dock Twelve, a pilot came scrambling up the Jacob's ladder, and the launch thundered away.

The ship was tied up for three days in Colombo. I got two bottles of Old Crow out of Captain Herre's bonded stock and checked into the Galle Face Hotel, a stately old pile outside Colombo, filled with British officers and their families. While buying newspapers in the lobby, I exchanged pleasantries with a slender English lady named Mavis. She accepted my offer of a drink in the room. We did not come up for air for two days. We did not exchange histories, but I gathered from indirect comments that her husband was a plantation owner. It seemed to me that Mavis was trying to prove that she was not past her sexual prime. That required a good deal of proving. She was a wizard at fellatio, and when she finally bowed out, I did not feel strong enough to crush a grape. My conclusion was that she had proven her point.

When the freighter headed out to sea again, south through submarine waters, all portholes and outside door passages were blacked out. Every night, our radio operator reported sinkings in the Indian or Pacific Oceans, and often, while I was standing on the dark bridge wings, the radar submarine-warning horns would squawk raucously. Staring out over the moonlit chop of waves, you could spot many emerging periscopes. Fortunately, none of them were real, and we skirted Fremantle, Australia, and powered through miles of orange weed underneath Down Under.

There was a nonstop poker game going on in the mess room. It was table stakes, and could get bloody. Bearing in mind that I knew neither the players nor the origin of the cards, I sat in cautiously. The two powerhouse players were Captain Herre and the navy lieutenant in charge of the gun crew aboard.

After rounding Australia, the freighter passed through Bass Strait and headed north for Hilo, Hawaii. After trying out the black-sand beach, Captain Herre and I moved into the Volcano House, a hotel on the slope below Kilauea. At the bar, we met a convivial Honolulu doctor who lauded us as unsung heroes and promised to assemble a luau that night in our honor, complete with authentic hula dancers.

That sounded promising. I unpacked my CNAC uniform and put it on for the first time; black whipcord with fine gold epaulettes, the Chinese airline insignia over the breast pocket, gold stripe down the trousers. I admired myself in the mirror extravagantly, thinking that I much resembled Douglas MacArthur as a young man.

The doctor appeared promptly with a small merrymaking mob and two lissome native dancers. I smiled indulgently on all this civilian foolishness until the doctor's wife brought me another drink. She admired my elegant comic-opera uniform, adding, "You people do get everywhere."

"Pardon?"

"General Motors. Isn't that what it says? GMAC, the automobile credit outfit?"

"No," I said stiffly. "It's CNAC, a Chinese airline."

As she stood with one hand on her mouth, I went to the bar for another drink or two.

Welcome home, warrior.

I HAD BEEN AN OPERATIONS officer for an airline flying through a combat zone, but I was a fake U.S. Marine. Oh, I got the full eight-week basic treatment at Parris Island, where they cut my weight thirty-seven pounds, the hard way, but I was never a true Semper Fi.

Before leaving Calcutta for the freighter trip home, I had written a letter to Frank Tolbert, an old friend of mine. He had been a columnist for the *Fort Worth Star-Telegram*, majoring in sketches of local sports characters such as wrestling promoters. His subjects came smoking off the page with full Hogarthian flavor and as much bite as the editor would allow him.

Tolbert was a Marine lieutenant and managing editor of the *Leatherneck* magazine, official publication of the Corps. Subscription to it was mandatory but unofficial. Of course, you don't *have* to subscribe. You don't have to do seventy-two hours on the parade ground in full field pack either. So *Leatherneck* had half a million devoted readers and its own building on K Street in Washington, DC. I wrote Tolbert that I was leaving the China airline and could probably help him fill up his magazine. I knew he would try to help because I had been selling stories to *Collier's* and the *Saturday Evening Post* and had aided Tolbert's break into those markets. He was close to being an original, in the Damon Runyon style.

Captain Herre, the Merchant Marine skipper of the *Cape Lambert*, had been astonished when his radio shack had picked up a personal message to me from Tolbert. The ship was blacked out and keeping radio silence on the final leg of its voyage between Hilo and San Francisco. The message was that, after reporting to my draft board in Fort Worth, I would be joining the next cadre of Marine Corps draftees. I would report to Parris Island Basic Training Camp as soon as possible, and after that report to the *Leatherneck* headquarters in Washington, DC, as a member of the magazine staff and combat correspondent.

One night I explained to Herre that if you controlled the personal publicity for Marine Corps generals, all things were possible. The skipper only grunted and dealt another hand. He had no bitch coming. I was not only his sole passenger, I was more than paying my way. By the time we passed under the Golden Gate bridge and docked, I owed him over eight hundred dollars from the poker game. He was kind enough to accept Pan American Airways checks I had earned in CBI [China Burma India Theater].

When I stepped off the Toonerville Trolley train, which ran to Parris Island in South Carolina, I found the Marine Corps waiting for me. They knew two main things about me that demanded close attention. First, I must be rich, because I had a story appearing that week in *Collier's*. More important, after I got through Parris Island training, I would automatically become a sergeant. In eight weeks. There were Corps combat veterans among the drill instructors who had been in the South Pacific for three years, veterans of bloody battles like Peleliu, who had never made it past corporal. Now here came this blond prick, after service with a pisspot Chinese airline, who was going to vault over them in rank after a few weeks' training. The inequity was glaring, and they could do something about it in the brief time they had me. They did.

The miseries of the recruit in a military basic training camp have been too well chronicled to warrant repeating. Mine were the same, only more so. Fresh off the little train, still wearing civilian shoes, we were stood at attention under a blistering sun and assured that we had come to the war too late to be a factor, that we could not possibly become real Marines. We were obviously the sweepings from a cowardly section of American society. Therefore our first chore, as despicable shitheads, would be to carry new mattresses to replace the tear-stained ones now in place at Parris Island. And, said our drill instructor emphatically, although we could never become real Marines, he intended to see that we became the mattress-carrying champions of the world. We did, too, on the run for over twenty hours.

I was lucky. Being nearly thirty years old, I could observe the drastic training process with something approaching detachment. At night, in the darkened barracks, you could hear eighteen-year-olds crying. Several hanged themselves.

There was also a constant floating population on the island which had gone AWOL from their training platoons. That may seem incredible, but it was possible because these recruits could tail in on chow lines and join work details without being detected.

Midway through the training, I learned that the photographer with whom I was to work as a combat team, Bob Sandberg, was also on Parris Island. He had been one of the senior photographers on *Look* magazine until the draft got him. We seemed to get on well together.

By the time our eight weeks were up, I had crystallized my impressions of the Marine Corps. First, their battle strategy always called for a frontal assault. The victor was on the side which sustained the most casualties. This, in turn, meant that every Marine under star rank had to stop thinking entirely, about everything. Secondly, the non-combat role of the Marine Corps was an unceasing publicity hunt, a constant self-glorification that cast the gyrene in a mythic role.

Because of these legendary qualities, the Corps made an ideal debt collector for American businesses all around the globe. It was principally so deployed in peacetime.

I did little to rock the boat. Once, while my platoon was in formation at attention, the DI said that to receive our mail we would have to break ranks and pick it up on the double, running. When my name was called I did not move and explained from a brace that every recruit had to be handed his mail, that delivery of it had no Marine Corps connection. I won that one, but at considerable cost.

My only other clash with authority came while I was holding my rifle at rigid attention. The DI snatched it, tilted the weapon for inspection, and carelessly flung it back at me. The bolt struck my forehead, brought blood, and fell to the sand at my feet.

The DI stared at me with hostile eyes. "Pick it up, shithead!" he ordered.

"Not in a thousand years," I answered. The platoon around me quivered.

The DI considered me for a few seconds, then ordered us back to barracks with the rifle still lying in the sand. Another recruit went back later and returned it to me.

WHEN I WAS RELEASED from bondage at Parris Island after eight weeks, which were the most effective reducing course ever invented, I moved into a suite in the Washington Hilton. Donning the dress blues which made me look like a real Marine, I declared the bar open to anyone who wandered in off the street.

One of those who did was George Polk, showing off his attractive Greek wife. Polk was an old friend of mine who had lived only a block from the Rivercrest Country Club in Fort Worth. In his teens, he had been mostly a blond Adonis type, seemingly untainted by intellectual turmoil. One day, this typical jock took off for Alaska. We had heard rumors of turmoil with his parents but nothing specific.

That sort of revolt was almost the norm among the children of country-club society. After a spasm of rebellion, they got tired of being broke and stranded and crawled back home for tea and sympathy. George made it stick. He worked in fish canneries in Alaska, bummed his way across Siberia and into Europe. Then he was in charge of the foreign desk of a major newspaper in New York, shifting from that to doing broadcast journalism for a network. He moved up like a rocket against the background of world war, his rough edges smoothed out and his mind becoming informed.

Not long after Polk assisted in the Washington revels in my suite, he was found floating in Salonika Bay, trussed and shot through the head. A minor legend grew up around him.

The most welcome visitor was my youngest brother, David. After desultory attendance at two universities, he had become a thespian, good enough to play junior leads in national touring companies. Uncle Sam had rescued him from grease paint. He became a turret gunner on a B-24 bomber. His flashiest part was when he had to parachute out of a burning bomber, hit by flak over Vienna. He was a POW in Germany for over a year.

I was working on the China airline when word came that he was missing in action, his plane shot down over the Wiener Neustadt ball-bearing factory. My mother cabled this news from Fort Worth but concluded, "He'll be back."

The Phillips brothers were adequately represented in the war. Edwin, the eldest, was still a Signal Corps captain in New Guinea. I was lately of CBI and beginning a career as Marine combat correspondent. Olcott, the heavyweight contender, had been declared an officer and automatic gentleman by Fort Sill, and David had bailed out of a burning bomber over Germany.

The K Street headquarters building of *Leatherneck* was half-zoo and half-normal. The editorial staff was filled with competent, even brilliant, writers and editors who could fill the pages admirably but made odd military types. We did have an obligatory officer of the day, wearing a sidearm against Axis invasion, but this rotating duty was a danger to us all.

We had illustrators of national reputation such as Tom Lovell. Frank Tolbert was managing editor, and on the staff were lesser lights from many magazines. Our undisputed lunatic-in-residence was Fred Lasswell, who had inherited the Barney Google comic strip and turned it into Snuffy Smith, which is still prospering and improving. Fred was an inept but persevering Casanova. His wife, who was considerably smarter, foiled every tryst he improvised. One memorable night she even pursued him through the K Street building, brandishing the Officer of the Day's pistol.

Because of its forced-draft circulation among the Corps, *Leatherneck* had over half a million subscribers and no problems in collecting from them. That meant money to spend. At first, I was the writer and Bob Sandberg, late of *Look*, the photographer on a combat team. Orders were cut, directing us to join the Okinawa invasion, and we were processed with that in mind. Just before it started, orders came down from Marine Corps headquarters cancelling our participation.

Tolbert called from Washington to say that someone had been reviewing the Okinawa plans and had noticed that I had just come out of the CBI theater. Frank assured me that the Corps was not really concerned about my immortal ass but didn't want it blown off after recently emerging from a combat zone. Semper Fi, kid. Bad publicity.

So what to do with this high-powered combat team which couldn't be allowed into combat because performance of one of its members, the writer chap, might backfire on the Corps' never-ending hype? While Bob Sandberg and I lolled around in the best bars and told plausible lies, this grave problem was mulled on high.

The result was the strangest set of orders ever turned out for enlisted men. Sandberg and I were issued a set of papers which allowed us complete freedom of travel anywhere in the continental United States, Alaska, and the Panama Canal Zone. We could choose any subject which related to Marine activity, including military hospitals. These orders were directed to all commanding generals and admirals, requesting that they give us all assistance and cooperation necessary to pursue our stories. Only generals usually got such travel papers.

When suitable Military Air Transport Service (MATS) flights were not available, we could buy first-class tickets on airlines. There was no restriction placed on our expense accounts. Time after time, commanding officers read through these orders and demanded to have a look at the team which had caused them to be written. One Navy captain with years of service looked us over, shaking his head, and muttered that somebody was stark raving nuts.

"Sergeant," he told me, "if you ain't a goddamned fool, you and your pal will go to Alaska and start a silver-fox breeding farm. Or mine for gold. Nobody will ever know."

King of the goldbrickers, I came to attention and flashed him a genuine salute. And often, in the cool of the evening, when the screwing began, I flashed a like obeisance eastward toward the unseen protector at Headquarters who had so strictly interpreted Marine public relations.

Our luck held. We interviewed people like Pappy Boyington of Black Sheep Squadron fame. In the living room of the sheriff of San Diego, Hank Adams, who had been a decorated Marine major, we watched his tiny Hawaiian wife do an eye-popping hula. Once, we were ordered to join a cruiser at Long Beach and ride her down through the Panama Canal and up to Norfolk while putting together a story on the Fleet Marine Force abroad. Although the voyage would be through peaceable waters, once again we were snatched off the assignment. The unwinking eye at Headquarters was still at work.

Since as the writer, I was first among equals on the *Leatherneck* team, Bob Sandberg often gave me the treatment. He had been a top magazine photographer for years and juggled his cameras with deft ease. Whenever we got into close quarters, which was often, he would have me crouch on a rickety table, holding the flash reflector like a poor relation. His deadpan commands to lower or raise the light would finally have me falling over backward. Anything to show the curious crowd who was really running the operation.

The only work of any quality we did on this privileged safari was in hospitals. Here, because of our remarkable orders and the always-present ego of doctors, especially surgeons, we put together a picture and text series on badly wounded American soldiers and sailors and the procedures and therapies being used to rehabilitate them.

One patient is never far from my memory. He was in a locked isolation ward, and no nurse or orderly was allowed to touch him. In our interview and photography session we were kept a barred, locked door away from him. The patient was a young man of moderate stature who appeared to be in good health. He had straw-colored hair, a diffident smile, and Appalachia in his tone. He could not have been more than twenty years old. He had been in the isolation cell for over a year because of his grotesque disfigurations.

At his neck, like a huge Elizabethan ruff, he had soft red wattles up to his ears, in layers, like a monstrous rose blooming. At his wrists and ankles there were smaller fungus growths of the same curious flowering. The doctor in charge of the isolation ward said he was not a military casualty. He had been on duty in a Filipino jungle detachment when the peculiar growths appeared.

Yes, he had been sexually active with the native women. But there were no other similar cases among his military comrades, and his blood tests did not indicate any venereal involvement. He had endured a steady drenching with penicillin and other antibiotics. Nothing worked. The growths did not increase in size, but neither did they decrease. He was in no pain except from lack of exercise and sunlight. The surgeons refused to cut into the growths, even for a biopsy, for fear of triggering carcinoma or something else.

The soldier trapped in the strange growths talked to us readily, but his doctors were more reserved. They had no diagnosis for him, nor any prognosis.

When we had contact prints on what Sandberg had shot past the barred doorways, I whistled at their excellence. Sandberg nodded and told me not to count on seeing them in *Leatherneck*. I asked indignantly why not. The poor bastard who could not even have his food handed to him was an obvious war victim. Regardless of where his fungus growths had come from, he was paying off at the end of the line.

"True enough," said Sandberg, "but you'll never see any of these tough pictures in print. *Life* and *Look* might have used them, but they sure as hell ain't what the Corps is selling."

An easier trip, and a great success in print, was the picture story we did on the wedding of the blind Marine corporal. We had him measured for a new set of dress blues and covered the bare location he was going to open as a convenience store in New Jersey. His childhood sweetheart was a shy little brunette who blushed on cue, and Sandberg did fast justice to the resplendent Marine color guard.

That one nearly folded on us at the last minute. The blind young groom cornered me while Sandberg was shooting and said that he wanted to junk the idea. "Why?" I asked. After the story appeared, he would be a minor celebrity and would inherit all the loot we had assembled as background material. "I know," the corporal said, "and then the news will come out that I'm a goddamned phony. I didn't get blinded in combat. Me and my friends in San Patricio were dicking off. When the palm wine ran out, a smart bastard located some methyl spirits, wood alcohol, and that's what blinded me and killed two of them."

That was bad news, and I wondered who the hell had tipped the story to us. The corporal had been on duty somewhere in the Hawaiian hinterlands when the wood alcohol interrupted a drinking spree. I told him that he was an unlucky fellow—also stupid, I thought, but did not add it—but that his loss of sight had been incurred while in the Corps. He was an authentic casualty and deserved any help we could scrounge for him, facing the darkness ahead. I advised him to keep his mouth shut and accept it.

He did, and we got a moving story. In the long run, Bob Sandberg was right. We never got a single picture or word of text printed on our coverage of the badly wounded.

MY DICTIONARY DEFINES Moloch as "a deity whose worship was marked by the sacrificial burning of children." While still in uniform, I had written an earnest little polemic against war for *Story* magazine. It was called "The Delegate from Everywhere" and featured a wounded soldier interrupting a UN meeting, displaying a limping, sightless group of war casualties. The delegate tells the great assembly that the trumpets are crumpled and the drumheads smashed.

To emphasize my complaint, trim, decent Harry Truman, the ex-bagman from Kansas City, ordered two atomic bombs dropped on unarmed civilian populations. The little haberdasher, without missing a drink or a poker hand, effectively negated any idea of the perfectibility of mankind. The idea of Jesus Christ became a discarded fable.

When the war in Europe was over, I put in for a hardship discharge and received one. My wife, Zen, had been having increasing circulatory problems in her hands because of Raynaud's disease and was on her way to the Mayo Clinic. When she had gone through the clinic, we moved to Mexico.

I could by this time, my thirtieth year, claim to be a writer. I had published two novels and a book of poetry, and my short stories had appeared in the *Saturday Evening Post, Collier's, American, Story*, and a few regional journals.

In 1946, we loaded the Buick roadster and aimed it at Laredo and the great plains of Tamaulipas: Zen, my beautiful ailing wife; Shawn, our three-year-old son; and I.

The dusty Buick rolled around the final turn to a small Mexican mountain village named San Miguel de Allende. The high air was clean and the streets cobbled. Our arrival there had been prompted by no more than a dropped remark at a Fort Worth party. A new art institute had been opened in the town. David Siqueiros was

Joyce and Shawn seen here just prior to her diagnosis of Raynaud's disease at the Phillips residence at 3725 Lenox Drive in Ft. Worth.
(UTA Archives)

said to lecture there, and Diego Rivera and JoséC Orozco were to come later.

After a week in the Posada de San Francisco, we leased a house at Numero 3 Calle del Dr. Ignacio Hernandez Macias. The place was a bargain. It was not a free-standing unit but one of a street of narrow, connected dwellings separated by twenty-foot walls covered by white and scarlet bougainvillea. The huge walls framed two patios, the rear one featuring lime trees and servants' quarters. The front patio was hidden from the narrow street by a large door which swung open to admit a car, with a smaller inset door for foot traffic.

The house was brand new and had never been inhabited. Downstairs were the *sala* or living room, a *comedor* or dining room with stained-glass windows, and a kitchen that burned charcoal. Upstairs were four bedrooms and three bathrooms flanking a columned terrace that opened on the sooty blue splendor of the Guanajuato mountains.

The price of all this splendor? Fifty-five dollars a month, and the builder of the place, "Loco" Sautto, was delighted to get a term deal on it.

Our way down from the border at Laredo had been eventful. After weathering the seared stretch to Monterey, we had paused in Linares to buy tangerines off the trees. Then we turned west off the principal Mexican highway, through the red-clay valley of corn and over the arid cactus desert to San Luis Potosi. The stone Aztec bridges, their surface pointed in the middle, had taken the oil pan off the Buick twice.

Given an unblemished white villa to decorate, Zen became a frenzied horticulturist. We went tramping through San Miguel's side streets on plant-buying tips, astonished Mexicans selling us vines and plants and root stock for what they considered imbecilic prices. A blacksmith got involved, put secure iron rings in the columns on the upper terrace. Begonias would hang from these rings.

The place became a riot of floral culture, flanked by huge *ollas*, pots, in the corners.

A local tinsmith was renowned for his lantern constructions, which were indeed clean, lovely designs. I bought two big ones from him and ordered two more, half the size, for bathroom use. He quoted a price for the small ones that was twice as much.

"Amigo," I said, "they only take half as much material and half as much time, so why the increase in price? *Demasiado*."

"No, *señor*," said the tinsmith. "Those little ones are tedious to make."

I knew then we were in the right place.

SHAWN, our three-year-old son, was a rampaging blond hellion. To his parents, he represented the major problem involved in the move to a foreign country. Could he safely drink the water, or cope with the problems he encountered playing in the street with Mexican children? We conferred with a local doctor who examined the boy, smiled, and said we worried too much. So we turned him loose. He cavorted with his peers, looking stunned at first when he could not get a comprehensible answer to a simple question.

One day, there was a noon parade in connection with one of the endless fiesta celebrations. We intended to take him down to the square to watch it, but he wouldn't go with us. Carmen, one of the maids, said she had promised to take him. Zen and I were in the crowded square, watching from a window in the office of a lawyer named Zavala, when the procession swept by, fired up by the tootling music of off-key cornets. Shawn was in the first row of the bannered marchers, riding on Carmen's shoulders and waving serenely to the spectators.

He learned kitchen Spanish with astonishing rapidity. A few months after we moved in, Zen had a tea party with finger sandwiches and pastry confections, a real high tea for the wives of local officials and friends who had been kind to us. The maids were in uniforms, and the whole tone was elevated. Shawn, tow hair plastered down and wearing unaccustomed shoes, was a principal exhibit.

One of the visiting *señoras* asked him how he liked his new Mexican friends. She asked the questions in Spanish and he replied in the same language.

"Felix is all right," he said, "but Jorge is a fucking goat."

I was working upstairs and hadn't heard these remarks. What I did hear was the burst of laughter from the *sala* as the starch went out of protocol and the party settled down to a gossipy level.

Not everything about our new life was charming. One of the

best features of San Miguel was a hot spring outside the town. After a night of tequila revelry, soaking in its waters was a sovereign cure for a hangover. The Taboada, as it was called, nestled in a grove of trees with picnic tables under them.

One afternoon, the three of us arrived to soak in the hot water and noticed an all-male group around one of the tables. At its head sat an old man who bragged about being one of Capone's gunmen in the old Chicago days. Lawyer Zavala had told me that the old man had lived there during the Prohibition period, but didn't know if his stories were true. Around this self-proclaimed ex-gangster were several younger men in *charro* clothes.

As we walked toward the bathhouse, one of them, obviously smashed to the gills, barred our way. He made Zen a drunken half-bow and flourished a .38 pistol, putting the muzzle of it between my eyes. He was so loaded I thought he might shoot me, just showing off. So I stood perfectly still, hoping that neither Zen nor Shawn would do any pushing or crying out.

After what seemed a long time, the old Chicago veteran barked out something from the picnic table and the swaying *charro* removed the gun from my head. The entire encounter hadn't taken more than seconds, but I had locked bowels for a few days.

Two weeks after I was frightened at the Taboada, I came downstairs one night to find Carmen, the maid, crying bitterly. I asked Zen what was the cause of the grief. She said that Carmen's father had been beaten to death last night, with rocks, on the road to the railroad station. He was a *pobre*, a peon. Somebody wanted his ragged shirt, or his worn huaraches.

The Mexicans had just cause for grievance against the gringo. Time after time, we had bullied them and our government had scorned them. Until recently, the country had only had one political party, the PRI, and it was enormously, pervasively corrupt. In 1940, in a highly disputed presidential election, the Mexican people appeared to have elected a former general named Andreu Almazán. The U.S. State Department, annoyed by his politics, promptly announced that it would not recognize him as president, and instead said that his defeated opponent was the president. Almazán declined to raise an army and revolt.

Several of my Mexican friends—a hotelkeeper, a lawyer and a doctor—said that they always voted. It was their duty, but they wrote in the name of their lowest peon for president, because no vote they cast would mean anything.

The Mexican idyll lasted two years. Comfortable in our bargain house, Zen and I managed a passable imitation of Scottie and Zelda, and our least remark got appreciative guffaws from company. We had a lot of company and served them lots of food and drink. Don Jackson, a friend from South Texas recently released from the Navy, cooked *cabrito* for us, and Beverly Thompson Jr. from Fort Worth, discharged from the Air Force as a major, flew his AT-6 down and stayed several weeks.

We went to see the mummies in the Guanajuato catacombs and the new volcano, Parícutin. One place I did not visit was the church at Dolores Hidalgo, where it was claimed there were 365 toilets, to be used in some ritual. The enormity of that stunned me. Here I had been peddling the idea of dedicating an airport with one measly fart, and this forgotten little Mexican church had hundreds of thunder pots. With that much rectal firepower, you could levitate the earth.

I was selling several stories a year, most of them to national magazines, so money was not a problem. The rent and payment to a cook and two maids came to about $150 a month. My view of the halcyon days was usually peaceable, lubricated by the good tequila La Herradura with the blue horseshoe on the bottle.

The Spanish say you must take what you want from life. Take it and pay for it. Two forces began to conjoin, forcing us out of the

San Miguel hacienda. First was the so-called Art Institute in the town. Because attending it got paid for under the G.I. Bill, war veterans poured in from the US. The second force was the progress of Zen's Raynaud's disease. Because she smoked almost frantically, the vasoconstriction in the blood supply to her hands threatened their tips with amputation.

Few of the veterans who came down to the institute had any interest in art. More and more they could be seen drunk in the street, often inert, and their behavior grew more lunatic. When one of them killed another, wielding a portable radio as a weapon, I knew the time had come. I drove the Buick to Mexico City with a Peruvian friend along, an hombre named Felix Rosas.

It was illegal for foreigners to sell their cars in Mexico. When something is illegal in that country, it just means the *mordida*, or little bite, goes up. Felix vanished into the bureaucracy with two hundred dollars of my US cash and in two hours came back with an impressive document stating that my Buick had been destroyed in a highway accident. That same afternoon we sold the car that no longer existed for three thousand dollars more than I had paid for it several years before.

Back in Fort Worth, Zen's physician father had her hospitalized for testing, and it was finally decided that she had to have surgery in Boston. An internationally famed orthopedic specialist named Smithwyck agreed to do a sympathectomy on her, and the three of us flew east to put her in Massachusetts General Hospital.

ZEN'S DOCTOR, FATHER, AND I stayed in the Copley Plaza in Boston and were rigidly polite to each other. He had never approved of our marriage in the first place and felt that my absence in India with the airline and service in the Marine Corps had exacerbated her condition. The Mexican adventure had further worsened it.

He came from a long line of New Mexican ranchers and was a physician with an orthopedic practice in several states. I had little defense against those qualifications. Yet in the treatment of his eldest child, my wife, he was permitting conduct which was indefensible medically. Zen had always carried a deadly pharmacopoeia with her: barbiturates, amphetamines, Percodan, Dilaudid. At the drugstores, she had *carte blanche* over his signature. On our trip to Boston, she took along a hypodermic spike he had authorized.

Raynaud's is a syndrome of idiopathic origin, occurring principally in females. The surgical procedure Zen faced required severing both branches of the sympathetic nerve in the back. This would release blood flow to the upper extremities, but the benefits were often only temporary.

Smithwyck and his staff were awesome to observe at work. A platoon of lesser medical workers moved behind him on rounds, taking notes. A pleasant Bostonian, he spoke in dicta of iron. Unless Zen agreed to give up smoking entirely, he didn't want to waste a bed and his time on her.

Secondly, Smithwyck said, he had no objection to her keeping bottles of Scotch or whatever other alcoholic drink she liked in the room. Tobacco was forbidden because it was a vasoconstrictor, but alcohol was permitted and welcomed because it was a vasodilator. So saying, like Moses from the mountain, the doctor swept out with his entourage following. It was not hard for a layman to see why he had been chosen to operate on an English king.

The operation itself went without incident. It was shocking to see the way blood mantled back into her blanched forearms and fingers. After a few days of recuperation, we flew back to Fort Worth.

AFTER ZEN HAD RECOVERED from the effects of her surgery I took a trip to Europe. Two projects were underway. One was a syndicated newspaper column called "Scene in Europe." It was intended for Sunday papers, short feature-story stuff with a humorous twist. While working in New York for Billy Rose, I had moonlighted a minor scam along the same lines, called "Scene in New York." The point of it was to puff columns on New York notables for publication in their hometown newspapers. It is a commonplace that people invariably want their hometowns to know how splendidly they are doing in the big world. I had a partner in this questionable enterprise, a guy named Al Durante, who was a nephew of the famous comic Jimmy Durante. Al worked for the *Daily News* and could always latch onto a Speed Graphic to grab pictures of the subjects. At one time, we had eighteen papers going for this pablum, including the *Fort Wayne News-Sentinel* and of course the *Fort Worth Star-Telegram*.

The second project was to gather background for an international crime novel on art thefts, based on Vermeer.

I got to the Port of London on the S.S. *Bassano*, a small freighter carrying eight passengers. One of them, my cabin mate, was Tommy Thompson, a correspondent for the *London Times*. The other passengers were Dutch or English. All deck-strolling on the *Bassano* was limited to the bow area. The ship was a coal-burner, her aft decks covered with a sooty powder.

There is not much to do on a freighter in mid-ocean, so after the passengers' most treasured lies are told, the rhetoric gets inflamed. Thompson of the *Times* was a cute bastard, and I awakened one hungover morning realizing that the night before I had promised to do a full turn that afternoon shoveling coal in the ship's boiler room.

Dante should have been with me. There were two gleaming red maws, one high and one low, and you delivered a shovelful of coal to each one alternately. The boiler room was so hot you had to strip

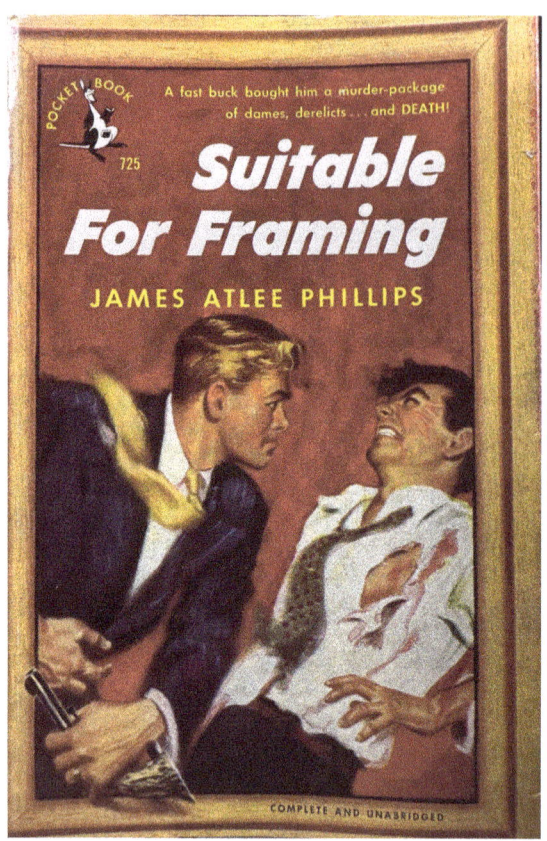

Conceived while writing his brand-new 'Scene in Europe' column for syndicated Sunday papers, this pulp thriller features a smuggled Vermeer, a Mexican general, eerie graveyards, lucha libre, and a terrific two-fisted cover. *(Author Collection)*

to stand in it, and after I had spent four hours swinging the shovel at those inferno openings, I had lost twelve pounds and most of my vital juices.

Not all, fortunately. There was a Scottish lady in her mid-thirties, trim and soft-spoken, who drank nothing but tea and was the second authentic nymphomaniac I have encountered. The British journalist and I spent alternate evenings in her cabin. The lady's name was

Hortense, and she was not only sexually insatiable but a contortionist. Thompson and I checked with each other, hollow-eyed, every day at lunch, and when her husband came to meet her at the London dock, we both waved good-bye with heartfelt relief.

I toured through Scotland, taking care to avoid Hortense's hometown. In Edinburgh, I asked a man in the street for directions to the post office and had no idea what he told me. I walked through Ireland in the countryside, and in County Cork came close to the area from which my paternal grandparents had sprung. They seem to have been principally pig thieves and rapists, with a strong bent toward poteen.

In Paris, I checked into the Hotel de Paris, a *luxe* establishment that ordinarily would have been far beyond my means. But before leaving Fort Worth, I had had a typewriter mechanic drill out the platen of my portable so that furled hundred-dollar bills could be secreted in it. There was no way the contraband currency could be detected without dismantling the slide carriage of the machine. In Paris, so soon after the war, US cash could triple the local money and be changed readily in any alley.

While living like a minor pasha, I encountered a Yank wild man who flew racehorses around Europe in his own plane. He seemed to know every *poule* in Montmartre. After a week-long blur of champagne and showgirls, his suite in the Meurice was locked up by the management, and he flew out of the country just ahead of his creditors.

After spending a week in Madrid at the Prado Museum, I backtracked to France and checked into a *pension* called Les Bananieres in the hills above the port of Nice. I was the only resident not fluent in French, but this was more a source of merriment than misunderstanding. I settled down to work on the art-crime novel. When I took a break, it was usually to Villefranche-sur-Mer, where Jimmy Jickles's bar offered suitable roistering. On one side trip, I visited Périgueux and learned about truffle gathering.

The "Scene in Europe" project failed. Before leaving I had printed up impressive-looking syndicate letterhead stock paper and had forwarded seventeen columns from my European ramblings, but somehow, between getting duplicated in Fort Worth and delivery to my New York agent, things had gone awry. Too bad, because it was a nice little dodge, and I had already signed up several papers.

The column failure freed me to work on the novel. In five weeks at the pleasant *pension,* I had done over two hundred acceptable pages. I was in the homestretch when I got a cable from Eddie-katz, my older brother.

> MOTHER HAS CANCER GOING NEW YORK TREATMENT
> YOU BOOKED CABIN CLASS SOBIESKI CANNES
> NEW YORK IN THREE DAYS PSE CONFIRM
> EDWIN PHILLIPS

When the Polish liner cleared Cannes, I was aboard, watching the Cote d'Azur recede. My mother was fifty-one years old; my father had died at thirty-seven. I had always resented her lack of observable flaws. Widowed but still beautiful in her thirties when my father departed at such an early age, she had become a successful businesswoman, civic leader, and art patron, and had turned down innumerable offers of marriage.

Staring at the whitecaps on the Mediterranean, I wondered how you helped a paragon die.

THE TRIP FROM CANNES TO NEW YORK aboard the *Sobieski* was the first I had ever taken on a cruise ship. In the next forty years, I would be a passenger on only one other. Although I preferred traveling by sea, except for these two trips it was always on freighters. After considerable study I arrived at a firm rule. When you have a choice, never take a ship of Italian or Greek registry. Any other European registries were acceptable, with the Scandinavians clearly superior. I suspect it is no longer possible to make the choices I had, because now it is nearly all organized party-time vessels, which I consider a boring abomination.

My voyage on the *Sobieski* was uneventful. Eating at my table was a tall young German girl who was a revelation in a bathing suit, and we lingered under the lifeboats at midnight. After the purser had been consulted and paid a small fee, I got access to the keys of the ship's laundry. At night, when that facility was not in use, we felt more comfortable reclining among the silent mangles and vats.

As we neared New York, the laughing German girl began to irritate me with her braggart anecdotes about high life in Berlin. Her father had a town house, a hunting lodge, a large powerboat, etc. I cautioned her about stressing all these worldly goods in New York. It might be resented, I said, because many New Yorkers were Jewish. The German girl clapped one hand over her mouth. "Oh, my God! I thought you knew I was Jewish. All those things were taken away from us."

My mother and younger brother, David, were living in a New York apartment in the Sixties, and I joined them. For several weeks we ferried a daily urine specimen to the office of an alternative-type oncologist in Brooklyn. He was called "Dr." Revici, a turtle-shaped little man reputed to be Rumanian. His cult-like following was based on injections of unknown substances, and he claimed miraculous cures. I have no idea where my mother had heard of him, but I suspect that she, being intelligent, had noted that orthodox treatment for cancer, with radiation and chemicals, was a Pyrrhic victory even if you stayed alive.

After a few weeks she had to move into a Brooklyn hospital. Her problem was a groin sarcoma. The anarchic cells were gnawing away at her right hip. When they reached the large artery there, the game would be over.

David Phillips, after his release from the POW camp, had returned to his acting career. He was matinee-idol handsome, and misfortune in the war had put some history into his face. He went out as a lead in the national road companies of two Broadway shows and, when not working, went through the usual rounds of cattle calls.

I was finishing the book I had been working on in France, and found it a pleasant relief one day when he said he wanted to take me to lunch. I agreed, and as we walked down the street, he said I should like the place. Great atmosphere.

"Oh? What's the name?"

"Cafe de la Temps."

When we got there, the cafe was an elaborate cafeteria. We joined the line and loaded up. David greeted several people as we sat down and there was considerable theatrical gossip, mostly about casting. By this time I was beginning to feel uneasy. After we had finished and were walking out of the building at ground level, I turned to stare back at the stone doorway.

David, watching me, was convulsed with mirth. The "Cafe de la Temps" was the cafeteria of the *New York Times*.

For a few more weeks we played out the farcical death watch. Maryllis grew steadily weaker but remained resolute. She had submitted to the unknown injections, preferring the unfounded hope they offered to the known burns and disfigurations offered

Surrounded by her children, Maryllis made the decision to stop receiving Dr. Revici's questionable treatments and expressed her desire to die at their family home. Seen left to right, David Atlee Phillips, Edwin Phillips, Jr., Mary Louise Phillips, and Olcott Phillips. *(Author Collection)*

by conventional medical treatment. She even had a new dental bridge built, costing seven hundred dollars, and it fitted nicely.

Finally, one late afternoon in Brooklyn, she told us that the Revici method was not working and that she wanted to die in her own house, near the redbird in her garden.

That decision gave us the blessed relief of action. Eddie-katz, the oldest brother, came up and tackled the New York Central Railroad. She was now so weakened that a window had to be taken off the side of a Pullman stateroom, and she was loaded into it on a stretcher, with a nurse in attendance.

A few days later she died in her own bedroom. I suspect that the attending physician, who had been her doctor for over thirty years, had assisted her out of pain, but I don't know if she got to see the redbird again.

The funeral was suitably impressive, I'm told. An elementary school was named for her and, by private subscription, a cancer research laboratory founded. She had been a member of the Fort Worth school board for a decade. After her will had been probated, I bought the other three-quarters of the family home from my brothers. It was a rambling wooden house with several outbuildings on a wooded triangular block near the country club.

I write these recollections at midnight in 1989, forty years after her death. Downstairs, an hour ago, I inadvertently tuned in to a television talk show of the toilet type. A loud-mouthed moderator was, as usual, inflaming his cretin studio audience. The subject of this night's mindless sensationalism was a bent old man, ninety-one years old. His name was Dr. Revici. He was the Rumanian quack who had attempted to treat my mother in 1947. He was still going strong. His medical license had been jerked and recovered several times. He was still fleecing the marks. I had to admire him. He couldn't help his patients, but he seemed to have solved the secret of long life for himself.

AT AGE THIRTY-FOUR I was back at Fort Worth, mired in the middle-class morality of that society. I had a large, remodeled house covering its own block and, like Candide, was cultivating my garden. I had a beautiful wife whose looks were beginning to fade, a rambunctious six-year-old, and a coterie of self-professed liberals.

The house itself was not much, but the grounds were excellent, with sufficient lawn and towering groves of trees. One end I let grow into riotous tangles of shaded shrubbery. As was fashionable, Zen and I drank too much. Both of us were heavy barbiturate users and had been for years. In addition, she had a constantly replenished arsenal of painkillers. Half my day was spent in writing and the other half in caring for the foliage, lawn, and trees.

I was selling everything I wrote. If the *Post* or *Collier's* wouldn't take a story, my agent would drop it down to *Argosy* or *Blue Book*. In our social romps, we ritualized condemnation of God, the Federal government, and on down to the High Sheriff of Tarrant County. We did not, however, have the guts to hunker down at the barricades for any causes. Between what I could make from writing and what we could leech off Zen's rich doctor father, we were amply funded.

Then, one midnight, I got a call from Manila. Loy Fal wanted me to run an airline for him in Burma.

Loy Fal was the closest the Chinese mechanics could come to pronouncing the name of Roy Farrell. When I had been handling operations on the China airline, in upper India, he had been an object of some derision along the flight line. A gangly pilot from Vernon, Texas, he was reputed to have flown nothing larger than a Cub before he reported to us, and the early line on him among the Chinese personnel was that he was most likely to be an early casualty on the Himalayas.

That did not happen. He got steadily better, and when the dangerous part of the Hump flight was over, he was among its leaders. When the rest of the pilots tried to re-enter civilian life in the States, Roy went to a surplus-aircraft depot and bought his own DC-3. He made it airworthy, got it licensed, and flew it back to China. Setting up shop in Shanghai, freelancing against people like the Soongs and Tommy Corcoran, he built up an airline and bought more planes.

When his operations were forced out of Shanghai into Hong Kong, he and an Australian named Syd de Kantz began a service to Australia. It too prospered and became Cathay Pacific Airways, still the dominant Asian carrier. When Farrell was forced out of its management because of his nationality, he promptly cranked up Macao Airways, which flew gold from that island to Hong Kong. One of the Macao planes was the victim of the first recorded case of aerial piracy. An air pirate shot the captain, and the plane crashed into the Pearl River.

Regrouping in the Philippines, Farrell set up his third airline, calling it Amphibian Airways. On this one he was using Catalina amphibians, PBY-5As. This line prospered briefly, then started fading until it was reduced to flying water buffalo around. But all the time, Farrell had his ear tuned to the pilots' grapevine. The new government of the Union of Burma had been formed in 1948, with U Thakin Nu as its head. The fledgling nation was socialist and peace-loving, a Buddhist model, but faced almost insoluble problems. The opposition was Communist but there was also an ongoing revolt by the people of the Karen region, and Chinese general Li Mi's Kuomintang Division was infiltrating north Burma after being driven out of Yunnan.

The railway system in Burma, once excellent, had been destroyed in the war against the Japanese. There was no navy for river or sea transport and no national airline. Farrell flew one of his Catalinas in and demonstrated that they could be used both in water and on land. He was offered a handsome contract for military transport charter, using four of the Catalinas, to move troops and ammunition and, principally, to show the flag of the new government.

Thakin Nu's regime needed such a demonstration badly. In 1947 the greatest Burmese patriot, Aung San, and most of his allies, who were known as the Thirty Brave Comrades, all of them trained in the Japanese war college, had been machine-gunned as they sat in a Cabinet meeting.

Two days after the phone call from Manila, I caught a plane for Rangoon.

AS I FLEW HIGH ACROSS THE PACIFIC, returning to Asia five years after I had left the Hump job, I meditated on Roy Farrell and the new job I was headed for. Pappy Farrell had been a slow start, but he had learned fast and was a bundle of energy. Because of its peculiar location and war-time limitations, the China flight had been one of the world's greatest smuggling operations, and Farrell had been one of the top hustlers of contraband.

Through connections with the flight-line mechanics in Calcutta, Dinjan, Kunming, and Chungking [now Chongqing], he had gold tolahs, penicillin tablets, firearms, and Swiss, English, and American cash stashed in wing spars and propeller hubs. The contraband had to be unloaded off the China side with a blowtorch. Even parachutes were packed with gold. And on the return flight, Chinese families sent out jewelry, museum-quality scrolls, and art objects.

The smuggling was no secret. The American C.I.D. was clocking it and could have busted nearly every pilot, on both the military transport flights and those on our China airline. When I had boarded the freighter to depart from Calcutta in 1944, a C.I.D. major had cornered me and said it was a patriotic duty to blow the whistle on Hump smuggling. I laughed and gave him a drink, saying that the only thing I ever saw smuggled was a bicycle, a brand-new one, leaning against boxes of dynamite. It was so shiny and obvious the Indian customs officials stumbled over it while they checked the manifested cargo.

Nothing was ever done about smuggling because it cut too high in the Kuomintang government. We had routinely flown boxes of French lingerie for Chiang Kai-Shek's wife and her coterie in Chungking, and lost several pilots transporting endless bales of phony currency.

Roy Farrell had been taking the shake and paying the cumshaw all over the Orient and down through Indonesia and the islands to

Australia. He knew, if any Yank did, the perils involved in working for the new Burmese government. It was socialist and therefore wouldn't please Washington. Burma had a common border with China, and a retreating Kuomintang division was infiltrating the Shan states. The main opponent of the Government of the Union of Burma was Communist, and of course there was the Karen revolt. And in what had recently been Cochin China, Uncle Ho was deploying his Viet Minh. I concluded that Farrell had better get his money quickly, before all these movements gobbled up his little fleet of amphibian planes.

I spent two days in Manila, conferring with Farrell, and flew on to Mingaladon Aeroport outside Rangoon. The field was under mortar fire when my plane landed.

A cheerful taxi driver charged me several rupees for the trip to the Strand Hotel in downtown Rangoon. He said there was no special significance in the attack on the airport. I had simply arrived too early in the morning. He explained that the Communist forces set off a fitful mortar barrage around the airport for two hours every morning while it was still cool, then knocked off for the rest of the day. That was my kind of revolt.

At the Strand Hotel, I was ushered into a suite with spacious balconies and arched doorways. Diaphanous curtains swelled in the breeze off the river below, and I could see children flying colorful butterfly kites. The rooms were served by tall, barefooted, noiseless servants in starched turbans with polished brass medallions set in them. The dining room waiters were even taller, Sikhs, and every table held damask serviettes folded into swans with spread wings.

It seemed a shame to leave that hotel, but I inventoried Amphibian Airways and found that there were three amphibian Catalinas at the airport, with a fourth flying in from Manila. There were four American pilots and ten Filipino mechanics. No office, no transport on the ground, no liaison between the airline and the offices of the Government of the Union of Burma, and therefore no contract to operate.

I met the pilots. One of them, Chet Brown, who had been a bush pilot in Alaska, lost no time in educating me. He was a tightly wound little man, quiet but emphatic, who did all his own maintenance, and said he would resign automatically if one of the Filipino mechanics ever put a wrench on the plane assigned to him. I agreed to everything Captain Brown stipulated because he was exactly what was called for on that job.

After renting office space at the airport terminal, I rounded up four Japanese carpenters and told them what I wanted, offering double pay for speed: a partitioned lobby office and a counter, two desks, and a wall of shelves for flight records. I insisted on their using the cheapest material available, like wallboard. The four Japanese gnomes deliberated and said wallboard was not available; it was imported and expensive. They would have to use a cheap local material, like teak.

I made a courtesy call on Win Pe [possibly U Thant], the Permanent Secretary for War, telling him that I had been sent by Captain Farrell and had written authorization to sign the charter contract for Amphibian Airways. The Secretary said that Mister P., an Italian con man who had been dabbling around the East since World War Two ended, had assured him that he, P., was the only proper signing party. I handed the perplexed Secretary my authorization, notarized in Manila, and said that I would be back in three hours.

I met P. in his Happy Valley house. Mountainous in the *longyi* skirt, which was accepted garb for men in Burma, he dressed me down severely for interfering in affairs above my station. I told him I was sorry, that nobody had informed me properly. P. said I was to meet him at the War Office the following afternoon at two. By then he would have alerted the proper officials. I agreed to this.

An hour later, back at the War Office, I signed the charter

flight contract for Amphibian Airways. Win Pe signed on behalf of the government of the Union of Burma. Three Burmese naval commanders were witnesses. The contract itself was a beautiful parchment document, engraved in pale green and hand-embossed with rampant green lions. For Farrell, the beautiful part was the hourly charter rate, which was higher than any previously paid to a civilian airline.

Our next requirement was for surface transport to get flight crews and machines to the aerodrome on schedule. The two major car agencies were still British owned, but I didn't seem quite the thing to them. They had no vehicles for sale and did not know when they would. I tried the second-hand markets but came up empty again. Finally, the small Lebanese manager of the Strand Hotel, who had once been a professional boxer, suggested that I try the Chinese.

Within three hours I had inspected and bought for cash two brand-new International station wagons. The price would normally have been outrageous, but it was a bargain for us. Standing by the two sparkling vehicles in the gloom of a dusty go-down in an anonymous quarter of Rangoon, I told the Chinese merchant that none of our people was familiar with the city's street geography, and that we would require two experienced drivers for the station wagons.

"Yes, yes," he said, and quoted me another big-league price. The station wagons, with dependable drivers, would be at the curb outside the Strand Hotel at eight o'clock the next morning. Our captains and European co-pilots would stay there, and the Filipino mechanics and flight crews would be in the Greene Hotel nearby.

The next morning, after the ritual mortar fire, I made a trial drive to Mingaladon and back. The route was littered with the hulks of wrecked and twisted tanks, left over from the bitter fighting in World War Two. The road wound around the staggering bulk of the Shwe Dagon pagoda, over three hundred fifty feet high, with a roof of solid gold leaf inset with precious stones. That huge structure, surrounded by smaller, spired stupas, was the center of Buddhist worship in Rangoon.

The fourth Catalina had arrived from Manila and was being serviced. I reported to the Burmese government that we were ready, and Major Perreira of the War Office gave me a sealed envelope containing the schedule. That was the pattern we followed thereafter. We usually carried troops and ammunition, and the Burmese soldiers were small, so we could pack a lot of them in.

We flew almost everywhere in the year-old Union of Burma: Myitkyina in the north, Akyab on the west coast, Bassein, Moulmein [now Mawlamyine], Mandalay, and Toungoo. Considerable small-arms fire was directed at the amphibians. The lumbering planes were a slow target letting down or taking off, but although we took hits in the wings and fuselages, none was brought down.

One of our captains, Dick Hunt, was captured on the ground at Toungoo by the Karens. Instead of threatening Captain Hunt, or even imprisoning him, the Karen leaders made him an offer he couldn't refuse. If he would use the plane to fly one mission for them, they would allow him to fly it back intact to Rangoon, the only stipulation being that he would then remove himself from the war. He flew a trip for them and came back to Rangoon, and we put him on the next plane out for Hong Kong.

The days rolled by. Every two weeks, I billed the War Department for hours flown and made a wire deposit to Farrell's New York bank account through the Rangoon branch of the Bank of Hong Kong and Australia. Our payments were in hard currencies: Swiss francs, British pounds, or US dollars.

Often, when our planes were being turned around at distant Burmese fields, the natives would load them with fresh fruits and vegetables, of which Burma was a cornucopia. Before the wars had wrecked the Burmese economy, the nation had exported nearly forty percent of the world's rice crop. The day came, however, when one of our planes flew back with several caddies of raw opium hidden among the gift vegetables.

I did not hear about the seizure of the contraband opium on our planes until early evening. When I did, I drove my station wagon to the residence of U Nu, the Prime Minister. Although my arrival was unscheduled and after hours, the dapper little man received me cordially. I told him that Amphibian Airways would make no more flights for his government until we were assured of a military guard at all destinations and inspection of return loads. The next morning I was promised these things by the Office of "Q" Movements, but that was inevitable. We represented the only link Rangoon had with its provinces in the civil revolt.

Our pilots kept bringing back reports from the Shan states about the continued encroachments of the renegade Kuomintang division in that area. They were setting up well-guarded opium laboratories and sending the gray poppy dough to Bangkok. This booming industry was backed by the Taiwan government and presumably by the CIA. From it grew the notorious Golden Triangle across north Burma and Thailand.

The civil revolt, like the Karens behind it, refused to take on the trappings of conventional warfare. Our station wagons were vulnerable in their constant passage back and forth to Mingaladon Aerodrome, and I was always tense, fearful of snipers, while making that passage. I sat beside the drivers as we passed flower-draped *zayats*, small roadside shrines which were everywhere.

One morning, returning to town, I glanced at one of the shrines and thought my fears were being confirmed. A native, naked except for a loin *dhoti*, was running at the speeding station wagon, carrying something heavy. I shouted at the driver and looked back at the running Burman just in time to get a pail full of water right in the puss. My assailant pranced away, laughing like a crazy man.

"Amok!" I thought, because several other little brown men were running at us. The driver, however, was smiling, and more pans and buckets of water were unloaded in my face. I finally cranked up the window and saw that the dousing operation was universal. Bus riders were being saturated where they sat, and small boys were spurting streams at pedestrians to universal mirth. The driver explained that it was the *thingyan* ritual, part of the Buddhist New Year celebration, and that the water-flinging would go on for three days.

General Ne Win was head of the military. He had been one of the Thirty Brave Comrades who had attended the Japanese War College with Aung San and had turned against the Axis forces when the tide of war shifted. He was one of the few to escape when the Burmese cabinet, including Aung San, had been wiped out by machine-gun fire in 1947.

AS AN ANONYMOUS STRANGER wandering briefly in their midst, I learned to admire the Burmese people. They were the cleanest in Asia, often smiling or laughing, and women had ranked high in their society for centuries. Because of their pervasive Buddhist beliefs, they would not allow the destruction of any life form, including rats or insects. Their basic unit of dress, the *longyi* skirt tucked in by a fold at the waist, was far more comfortable as male attire than trousers.

As a boy in Texas, I had marveled at the legends of elephant armies and had viewed myself as principal mahout when the great beasts shuffled toward the enemy. I never managed that in Burma, but when one of our Catalinas ran off the runway in Moulmein, I got to hire an elephant to pull it out of the muddy ditch.

The English-language paper in Rangoon was a source of wonder to me. One day it carried a story saying that a Burman had been found in the bottom of a well, cut into four pieces. Solemnly the editor added a line to the story, saying that "the police suspect foul play." Around the great Shwedagon pagoda there were clusters of small business ventures run by monks in saffron robes. One blurred picture showed a tan lemur loping away naked from the pagoda. The caption over the picture was "UNFROCKING THE BOGUS MONK."

So as to avoid ambushes at the ends of our daily flights, I did not receive the flight schedules until the night before and did not announce them until we were actually on the flight line at Mingaladon field. Therefore I was not prepared for the flight schedule handed me one evening in a sealed envelope from Major Perreira's Office of "Q" Movements.

The message was unlike any we had received. It said simply that at ten o'clock the next morning our best available plane with our top flight crew would fly a living shoot of the great bo tree from Rangoon to Mandalay. After sanctifying the plane, a party of eight *bonzes*, monks, would accompany the little plant.

I called Eddie Law Yone, a local reporter, scholar, and publisher, and asked him to have a drink with me. Eddie, who was Burman-Chinese, confirmed the news. The Lord Buddha, Prince Siddartha Gautama, had been born in Nepal. Unlike Jesus, he was not of humble beginnings but was the son of a king. After a princely and dissolute life, he began his meditations at the age of twenty-nine. The place where he started his reflections, and thus his religious movement, was the shade of a peepul tree in Buddha Gaya [Bodh Gaya] in India. Twelve centuries ago, a shoot of this tree had been transplanted to Anuradhapura in Ceylon. Now, in the middle of a civil revolt, our little ramshackle airline was being asked to transport a shoot from the Singhalese tree to the monastery in Mandalay. It was no time for an engine failure.

The next morning at dawn, we pre-flighted the assigned Catalina twice and gave it a comprehensive check. A cavalcade of saffron-clad monks arrived at nine, two festooned jeeps leading the parade.

The shoot of the bo tree was a slender green branch in a tall golden bowl. The chanting monks swarmed over the amphibian plane, and a minor crisis ensued when the abbot insisted that the little tree must be carried ahead of everything else on the flight, even the cockpit and control panel. This problem was solved, and at exactly ten o' clock the curved hull lifted off the pierced-plate runway and circled over the gleaming spires of the great pagoda.

The flight north to Mandalay was uneventful. As a failed Episcopal choir boy and working agnostic, I realized that this was the least martial mission in which I had ever been involved, and prayed with all my heart that the little tree might prosper in its new home.

After ninety days of intensive flying activity, the government of the Union of Burma ran out of acceptable foreign currencies and the activities of Amphibian Airlines ceased. For another two weeks, with the consent of the government, we flew private cargo trips at a profitable rate but were paid in rupees. Finally, the four amphibian planes and all our equipment were sold to Burmans and the pilots and mechanics returned to their own countries.

We were lucky, and it was time. The whole operation had been a turnkey enterprise. No one was hurt, and we had no crashes. It was time, because in 1949 a little round-faced man from the caves of Yenan [Yan'an] drove Chiang and his Kuomintang profiteers to Taiwan and returned China to its people.

Farrell and his little flying circus, a free-enterprise anachronism, came close to being trapped in the closing jaw of Asian history. Mao and the Communists took over at the northern and eastern boundaries of Burma in that year. And a wispy-haired zealot called Ho Chi Minh, who had been setting up revolutionary cadres for twenty-four years, would surround the French at a place called Dien Bien Phu.

And not many years past that bloody event, ignoring its lesson, came the American blunder into Viet Nam.

PART THREE

THE WANDER YEARS

ONCE AGAIN, LIKE A YO-YO, I returned to Fort Worth. The place is a drag, and when I am there, I have a sense of loss. Once, not so many decades ago, men on horses rode through a wilderness without roads or boundaries and stopped at the bluff overlooking the Trinity River. "This looks likely," their leader said. "Let's stop here." They had ridden through grass belly-deep to a tall horse, and they founded another outpost in a burgeoning Yankee empire. Now I lived among their descendants and found them foolish and pretentious. I wondered if it was to be my karma to live there all my days, practicing my drinking until I got it right. Gentle Jesus, I hoped not.

I was selling almost everything I wrote to the top markets, which meant that it was carefully contrived, sanitized garbage. My seven-year-old son was a rambunctious delight, but my wife Zen and I were clashing because I thought her friends were fools.

As a relief valve I dreamed up a Caribbean jaunt, one in which I would roam from Cuba down through the Leeward and Windward Islands. Another feature story series for Sunday papers, with pictures I would take. This venture flopped too, because I emphasized things like leper colony lazarettos.

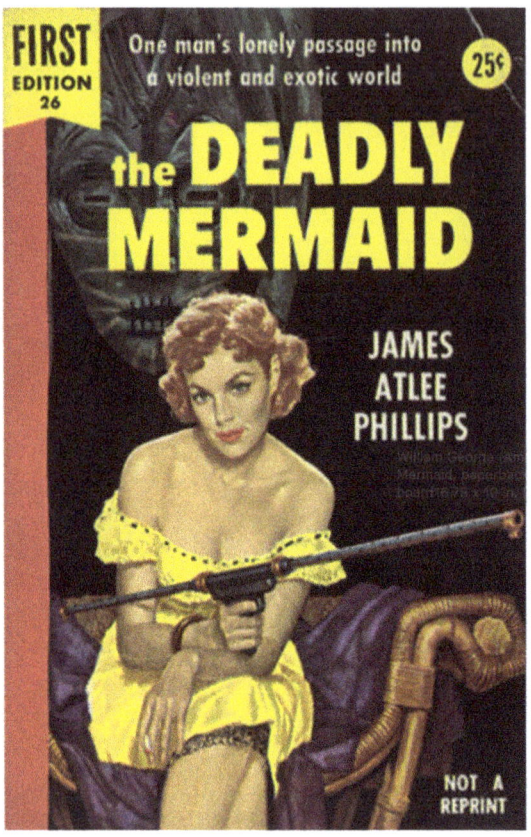

Two failed ventures—a feature-story proposal on the exotic Caribbean for syndicated Sunday papers and an unrealized narrative script for an ambitious underwater documentary in Haiti—nonetheless resulted in this terse tropical thriller with a classic pulp femme fatale on the cover. *(Author Collection)*

I was on my way back home when I met Alan in the lobby of the Nacional Hotel in Havana. Alan was a Fort Worth resident, one of the heirs to a wealthy family, and reputed to be an expert horseman. He was several years younger than I, a friend of my younger brothers. A handsome, hard-driving boy, he was a notable jug hound and, like so many of the country-club inheritors, trying to create an individuality for himself.

Alan was taking a crew of four to do an underwater movie at Caracol Reef, in the waters off Cap-Haitien, a city on the north coast of Haiti. Up in his suite, he showed me the orange Fenjohn underwater camera they would be using, and said it got fantastic color. Would I come along at his expense to join the scuba safari and, if they got footage to justify it, knock out some kind of story outline to make a documentary?

I flew with them to Port-au-Prince, then to Cap-Haitien, and the party settled into the Roi Cristophe Hotel. We worked the reef several hours a day, gained local approval by bringing in heavy loads of fish for the hospital, and wound up with several hours of strikingly beautiful underwater footage: teeming schools flirting around the white reefs and over the white sand, barracuda kills thrashing right into the camera, and an enormous leopard ray big as a rowboat pulsing overhead.

After screening it, Alan flew the whole party to New York and we took two suites in the Plaza. What was needed next was somebody who could organize the sparkling footage so that it made sense when coupled to surface activity. I called Bob Sandberg, the photographer who had worked with me in the halcyon Marine Corps days, and explained our problem.

Sandberg said he might know someone who could help, a young photographer on *Look* magazine's staff named Stanley Kubrick. He had shot a couple of movies on his own and was reported to be innovative. Kubrick came to the Plaza and screened one of his efforts, which did not impress me. It seemed to be shot in natural light, with people clutching trees, and probably had nuances I could not understand. Kubrick studied the possibilities of the underwater footage for several days, then said he couldn't help and withdrew.

After a week of skirmishing, during which I put together an outline and treatment, the documentary summit turned into a homosexual *bal masque* featuring soprano shrieks and nasty spats at midnight. I flew back to Fort Worth without disturbing the celebrants.

MY STUDY, HIGH IN THE BIG wooden house, was a good place to work. It was remote enough from the bedrooms of my wife and son so that the sound of my typewriter would not disturb them. Light from my study window fell across the swaying tops of wind-blown trees in the big yard. After my return from Burma, one evening long after midnight, I was working on a novel when the phone rang.

"Did you write that golf serial in *Collier's*?" a brusque voice inquired. I admitted authorship. "Good job," said the caller. "My name is Layne Britton, calling from Los Angeles. I'm a movie producer..."

A drunk movie producer, I added to myself, because the caller's voice had a breathless and wheezing quality.

"And I've got some people here interested in filming it. Is it possible to buy an option on the story?"

"Always," I answered. I had written sports stories for the *Saturday Evening Post* and *Collier's* for several years—baseball, football, basketball, rodeo, ranching—but had taken note that few golf or tennis movies had ever been made. "Tell me, Mr. Britton, do you always do business at this hour?"

"Real busy," my caller wheezed. "Gonna talk to my people and get back to you." He hung up. Since he had only announced an interest and had not mentioned money, I marked off the late call to party time and went on with the novel, which was set in Burma and got published as *Pagoda* in 1951.

A week later, at about the same lonely hour, Britton called again. He was still breathless, almost shouting, and still drunk. "I got RKO backed into a corner on that golf story. They'll buy an option, but they may try to stiff me on the deal. Will you piece me out if they close a deal on it?"

"Mr. Britton, my agent hasn't mentioned it if anyone out there is interested. If a sale for the option goes through, certainly I'll remember your participation."

"Okay." He hung up.

Three weeks later Zen and I were holidaying in Manzanillo, Mexico, when I was summoned from the beach to answer a New York call. My agent told me Sid Rogell's office at RKO had offered $10,000 for an option on "Just Like I Hate Money," the *Collier's* golf serial. Would I accept?

"Jesus, Max," I answered, "it's like finding a bird's nest on the ground. Call them back immediately."

In another two weeks, I had the check for ten thousand, actually nine thousand, thanks to my agent's 10 percent commission. RKO was then the property of Howard Hughes, and it pleased me to dip into his vast till. I called a friend who was in the story department at Paramount and got a rundown on Layne Britton. He was better known as Shotgun and was a minor legend, having emigrated to Hollywood from west Texas a decade earlier. He had been an outstanding football player at Hardin-Simmons College and, through some strange alchemy, had become a movie makeup man. He was not a shy man. He had worked on Crosby, Sinatra, Tony Martin, Mitchum, and most of the top feminine stars, and was reputed to be a special friend and protege of Jane Russell. He was an arm-waving drunk and a golfing fiend, who spent most of his free time touring the Hillside course, often with celebrities like golfers Ben Hogan and Jimmy Demaret.

After getting his home address in Long Beach from a phone directory I mailed a check for twenty-five hundred dollars to Mr. Britton. I had never seen the man, but after all, I had never seen Sid Rogell either, and Sid had sent me a check for nine thousand dollars.

A few days later Shotgun was again wheezing at the other end of the line. He thanked me briefly for the check, then said Bob Mitchum would like to talk to me. His hectoring tone seemed to be accusing me of deliberately wasting millions of dollars we could be making if I weren't so lazy. This, of course, sounded like more grand con, until he put Mitchum on the line. They were talking from his dressing room.

I greeted Mitchum and said that I didn't mind coming to the Coast, but what did we have to talk about?

"Oh, Christ," he answered. "Come on out. We'll think of something."

A week later I arrived at the Los Angeles airport and was met by Shotgun Britton. He was about forty, a bubbling, gasping man of constant movement and speech who smelled like a distillery. He would have been handsome if he had shaved. We nearly drove to the Beverly Hills Hotel in his little red Singer car. Nearly, because while driving at speed, he shifted inadvertently into reverse and the little car bucked to a halt and brooded over some shed parts.

At the nearest filling station, he talked the proprietor into towing the grounded vehicle and ferrying us into the grand curving drive of the Beverly Hills Hotel. Upstairs, I learned something else about Shotgun. In addition to frequent nips in the hotel bathroom, he was a human slop jar. He chewed tobacco and spat amber fluid on everything except the overhead light fixtures, all the time talking about the great possibilities in Mother Goose Land. As he harangued on, I unpacked and wondered how the great ladies and sweet ingenues of filmdom could stand the impact of this brown-stained, nonstop man. He was not a dainty object.

On the other hand, everywhere Shotgun Britton went was a noisy triumphant progression. Everyone from waiters to studio heads knew him and called him Shot or Shotgun. The maitre de in the Polo Lounge, which Britton loudly called the Polio Lounge, chatted with him. The doorman at the Beverly Hills started smiling when Britton approached.

Unannounced, he next took me to see Jean Simmons and Stewart Granger at their poolside. Pat O'Brien and his wife greeted him affectionately. That afternoon, when I met Dorothy and Robert Mitchum at their Mandeville Canyon home, Shotgun introduced the actor as the only star with a face shaped like a motorcycle seat. Mitchum smiled when Britton asked him to break out the pot sticks. It had not been very long since the actor had been jailed for using the noxious weed.

Shotgun took me to all these places like an eccentric uncle. I realized he was doing it to impress me, and I was impressed.

I FOUND MITCHUM, at home among his family, an amiable and literate man. His living room was littered with advance copies of books. Jim, his oldest son, gave me a demonstration ride in his brand-new Thunderbird coupe, scorching the bends on Mandeville and adjoining canyons. The Mitchum residence was a comfortable place, and Dorothy supervised it expertly.

Mitchum had a bottomless well of wry and wicked anecdotes and recollections of his journey to stardom. These carefully shaded stories were obviously well-rehearsed set pieces, covering his career from astrologer's shill to chain-gang escapee in Georgia to intimate glimpses of foreign princesses. Unreeling the tales, he incited his audiences to laughter, tears, and wonder. But his own eyes, appraising, never changed expression.

Set in a big head, they were the eyes of a Danish-Blackfoot mix, always wary. His shoulders were so muscular that he could put on a new shirt of the proper size and burst its seams by tensing and expanding his upper torso. After a few days, I began to realize he was claiming fraudulent proficiency in many small arts and sports. He had played so many parts that he had come to believe his old dialogue. Later, I would learn that this trait was common to many headline actors. In learning many roles, they would pick up the basics of a small dexterity and promptly discard it when the movie was over.

Mitchum's idea was that most of the good stock-car drivers came from the Big Smoky area of the southern United States, that they learned to be good drivers delivering loads of illegal whiskey, hauling it down from the stills to the city markets. He felt that a good movie could be made out of these moonshine boomer boys. I agreed, said I would try to figure out what we needed to make it workable, and flew back to Fort Worth.

My Burmese novel was published by Macmillan and adapted as an hour-long live television drama on *Studio One*. Six months later

Phillips's wealth of experiences in China while running daring air supply missions over 'The Hump' served as inspiration for this high-flying noir-thriller, featuring the first appearance of Phillips's superspy Joe Gall, albeit in a nascent form. *(Author Collection)*

I was phoned by Bob Fellows, the producer at John Wayne's new independent company called Batjac, who told me said Wayne was interested in *Pagoda*. Would I fly out at their expense to discuss it with him?

Since Wayne was the top box-office draw in the movie business, I said I would be delighted to come out for a talk. In the next year I made several flights to Los Angeles and began to fancy myself an impresario. It was on my first trip for Batjac that my old boyhood chum R. had put the erotic grope on me in the Town House. I even wrote on spec a detailed screenplay of *Pagoda* and delivered it to the Duke. Then I waited, making preliminary notes on Mitchum's reckless young men driving moonshine in the mountain passes.

Finally I realized that while I was an important-looking traveler with impressive destinations and all expenses paid, I wasn't actually making a dime. Jane Russell, whom I had met through Mitchum, did kidnap me once for a trip to meet her mother, a lay preacher, exhorting the faithful in her own church. I had published a story in *Collier's* called "The Wife Who Lived Twice," and Jane liked it. The story was a real weeper, a three-handkerchief job. After a Yankee wife dies suddenly while vacationing in Mexico, a blind peasant girl is given corneal transplants from her eyes and recovers her sight. It was the first fictional use of eye surgery. Russell said that nobody was writing for women anymore and pestered Howard Hughes to film it at RKO. Nothing came of that either, except that her mother prayed for me.

In 1952, I put four stories in *Collier's* alone and therefore could afford to shuttle back and forth, looking important with my movie connections.

A few of us were mildly whooping it up in Mitchum's dressing room at RKO one afternoon. The bar had been open for some time, and Mitch was instructing Jane Russell about something or other. The dialogue in his dressing room was nearly always superior to that being spoken on the sound stages. At that time, Dale Robertson was playing a lead in a Turkish period piece, wearing pantaloons and slippers with curling toes. The Oklahoma cowboy playing a pasha, twanging away at Turkish military orders, was a strange and wonderful sight. Jane was being fractious, which she could be when fueled by martinis. She was replying angrily to something Mitchum had said when there was a murmur from the window.

Vincent Price was leaning down to peer into the window, making the immemorial Catholic gesture with a forefinger. He was fully made up and had been on his way to a nearby soundstage.

"Oh, shit!" shouted Russell.

Price staggered back, his face frozen outrage. "Don't *say* that word, Janie," he pleaded, still backing away. "It's the trademark of an impoverished vocabulary." Tutorial dignity offended, he proceeded toward the set still shaking his head.

It had been one of his better cameo bits, and we all applauded. While we were working on the next round, a call came from Honolulu. It was for me. John Wayne was calling from the Edgewater Beach Hotel. He was ready to start principal production on his first independent film. All the actors and crews were already in the islands with him, the necessary equipment was in place, and the financing was committed.

"But I got a problem," said Wayne. "We haven't got anything to shoot. My writer promised he'd stay at least a week ahead, but he's blown a gasket. Hasn't drawn a sober breath since we got here. Spends all his time in the hotel bar, and when I try to reason with the dumb bastard, his only comment is 'I hope you get cancer.'"

The Duke added that it was costing him about $26,000 a day just to keep everybody housed and fed, and he couldn't stand much more of that. Could I fly over and try to help them keep ahead of the cameras?

"On my way," I said.

Wayne, over the years, had built up a repertory company of supporting actors such as Ward Bond, and the same production cadre was usually around on his films. The picture they had scheduled was called *Big Jim McClain*. It was the usual Commie-basher, a politico western with palm trees instead of cactus and car chases instead of running horses.

When I landed in Honolulu the next day, Wayne met me and asked what we could do to get his company moving. The first thing was to get a copy of Stephen Vincent Benet's story "The Devil and Daniel Webster" from the University of Hawaii library. We would open with a tracking shot over a concrete platform and then tilt it into the water to read the name of a sunken warship, U.S.S. *Arizona*. Then the dripping camera would emerge from the water and track through a New England forest, storm thrashing its trees and lightning rupturing the dark sky. As the camera prowled on through the storming forest and came to a solitary ornate gravestone in a clearing, a quiet voice-over would explain: "When you come to the grave of Daniel Webster and are asked the question 'Neighbor, how stands the Union?,' you had better be able to reply that the Union stands as she always has, copper-bottomed and solid, or that old man will rear right out of the ground." A sudden blinding white explosion illuminates the shaking gravestone. We fade to black and then segue into the credits and opening scene. Wayne was delighted. While this opening was being shot, I was given a suite and two secretaries and dictated undistinguished continuity for two weeks. Wayne began doing what he did so well, protecting democracy from the beasts of foreign ideology, slipping into that role like a comfortable coat. What resulted was an atrocious film, but that didn't matter. In the hinterlands, they came to see Wayne.

Off camera he was a considerate host. We split several bottles of sour mash, and I attended a polo game with him. From his partying in Honolulu society, he had somehow met an Ohio cousin of mine, a matron in her thirties. We had the usual persiflage about kissing cousins and mock threats from her red-headed husband. The Batjac company was leaving for location work in Maui, and I was invited to join them. I declined and made reservations to fly back to Los Angeles.

The first production from John Wayne's independent production company, 'Wayne-Fellows' (later 'Batjac'), 'Big Jim McClain' also achieved cult notoriety for its propagandistic 'red scare' themes and camp tone, especially Phillips's dramatic story opening repurposing of Stephen Vincent Benet's 'The Devil and Dan'l Webster.' *(Free Use/Public Domain)*

Wayne asked me how much they owed me and I said nothing. The opening I had written ought to work, but the rest of it was just nonsensical, brainless chase stuff. On the flight back, I admitted to myself that I was only stoking my vanity. I wasn't hurting for money, but that was not involved either. How many people got to give the ranking box-office star in the world a gift?

Batjac lawyers were waiting when I changed planes in Los Angeles. They too wanted to pay me for my work in the islands. With natural barrister prudence, they didn't want any potential claims hanging loose. So I accepted a dollar, signed a quitclaim, and flew on to Fort Worth.

I should have gone to Maui instead. Zen had filed suit for divorce. After one drunken outburst, when I called her lawyer and threatened to come down to his office and belt him over his desk, the legal machinery rolled on. Since her lawyer was six feet four inches and weighed 240 pounds, I must have been completely witless as well as intoxicated. Her right to a divorce was indisputable. I only came home to change clothes, and that's not very often.

During a tennis workout at the country club, I met a yachtsman who had recently sailed a single-hander from the Riviera to Trinidad. He mentioned seeing a snow-capped peak in the Canary Islands. For some reason that thought seemed incongruous, because I had always classed the Canaries as at least semi-tropical. I went to the Britannica and read about those islands.

For no special reason I decided to move to the Canaries, which were reputed to be the place where the dead heroes of the Greeks went to dwell. What was good enough for dead heroes seemed appropriate for me, so I began packing.

> THE ISLAND WAS FILLED with elemental midnight noises. I stood motionless on the terrace of the villa, sorting out the wild symphony. Far below my high eyrie the ocean waves were pounding the black-sand beach, smashing themselves to foam on the moonlight littoral. All around me the wind freshening off the sea was slatting banana fronds, fraying their edges. I didn't care. They weren't my bananas.
>
> Behind me in the glass-walled *sala* only the dials of the big high-fidelity cabinet were visible. From its three-throated speakers the Beethoven Fifth was thundering out defiance of nature's contrapuntal themes.
>
> Going to the corner of the wind-swept terrace, I looked up at the snow-capped peak dominating the island, the Pico de Teide. Once, on Ptolemy's maps, it had marked the west-

ernmost edge of the known world. The Greeks of his time had thought these Canary Islands the Elysian Fields, where dead heroes came to dwell.

Puerto Cruz was a warren of crooked streets and dim lights below, a half-African, half-Spanish fishing village where no one fished anymore, a haven for sullen chill-eyed natives and unwashed priests in rusty black, a cheap holiday resort for scrubbed Swedes quacking like ducks and a parade ground for bull-necked bad-mannered Germans shoving their way arrogantly past wan English residents kept permanently listless by island fever.

Those four paragraphs were an introduction I later used in a novel about the Canaries.

After I had landed in Santa Cruz, the principal seaport and largest city of Tenerife, I checked into the Mencey Hotel. There was a letter waiting for me. I was mildly surprised, because only my lawyer brothers in Fort Worth and my agent in New York knew about the trip.

The letter was from Millard Nash, a former Himalayan pilot with the China airline. He had flown several hundred trips over the Hump and was one of the best pilots we'd had, but he had stayed too long in the Orient. When he wrote the letter he was confined in a prison in Taiwan, serving a long term for smuggling drugs into Taipei.

Nash's scrawling handwriting was hard to read. He said he was trying to smuggle the letter out, was at hard labor with the other prisoners, and had lost nearly forty pounds. That bothered me more than the rest because he didn't have the body frame for that kind of loss. I cabled my brother Edwin to approach the State Department for information on the case.

Nash's arrest at the Taipei airport had been a fair catch. The plane he had flown in from Hong Kong was filled with contraband, principally wall hangings, and the wall hangings were filled with narcotics. I imagined he had paid cumshaw to the wrong officials.

My first letter from Tenerife, the principal island of the Canaries, was to John Wayne at his Batjac office in Los Angeles. In the letter I said that if he felt he owed me one, to call the baldheaded President and ask him to look at the sad case of the Yank imprisoned on Taiwan. That Nash was guilty as charged, but that he had been an extraordinarily fine pilot over the most dangerous flight route in World War Two. I never received any confirmation of receipt from Wayne or his office, but in less than six months Nash was freed from prison and returned to the States. The Duke and Eisenhower were good friends.

After I had mailed the letter, I went house-hunting. I got a car and driver and circled around Tenerife to the western side, past Los Rodeos—probably the most dangerous airport in the Western Hemisphere, obstructed at both ends of the runway—and past La Laguna to Puerto de la Cruz. Our vehicle was often trapped by road jams featuring obstreperous camels and antique carts. We stopped to view a locally celebrated dragon tree, reputed to be the oldest tree in the world, and came at last to the little port opening on the Atlantic.

Puerto Cruz was nothing special, but the road down to it skirted the Vale of Orotava, a fair valley of flowering plants and trees. There was a legend to go with it. Alexander von Humboldt, the famous German naturalist and world traveler, is said to have rounded the turn into this vale and dropped to his knees in astonishment at its beauty. The winding road to the port passed an extensive botanical garden.

Stopping for a glass of wine at an outdoor cafe on the beach, I looked up past Orotava at the Pico del Teide, over twelve thousand feet high. It was not now snow-covered, but I could make out pumice fields near the crest. My gaze came down from it and was caught by a white villa standing alone, directly above the little port.

The place looked like a stage set.

"Who owns that?" I asked the proprietor of the cafe. He informed me that it was the property of a German named Enrique Trenkel, who also had several *fanegadas* of bananas, a chief export of the island. I got back in my car and drove to his house. Don Enrique was a wiry and extremely polite little man who showed me through the bluff-top villa. Members of his family had recently moved out of it to go to Spain—the Canaries were an autonomous community of that country.

The furniture in the villa was dark and depressing, Teutonic horrible, but the two-storied place was balconied on the top floor, on the seaward side, and the huge *sala* had sliding glass walls. Halfway through the inspection tour I asked Trenkel for a figure covering a year's lease, with an option to renew for the same period. When he stated a figure, I agreed and paid him with traveler's checks. A long-lens shot of the villa appears on page 521 of *National Geographic* for April 1955.

Nobody had sent for me, and I knew no one in the Canary Islands. The first order of business after I had moved into the villa was to learn what I could about the little seaport below and the flowering valley above the house. The strange, twisted dragon tree, three thousand years old, was nearby. An infusion made from its seeds had helped in the embalming process used in the mummies found in island caves, which were second in quality only to the Egyptian. There were no specimens on local display. They had been stolen long ago and sent to museums in Rio.

Another anthropological puzzle was the origin of the ancient Guanche inhabitants of the islands. Tall and blond and some seven feet tall, they seem to have been Norse giants who overshot Europe, but the question has never been settled. A Harvard professor named Earnest Hooton came to Tenerife to study the problem but could never solve it.

The inhabitants of the nearby island of La Gomera had developed a whistling language which could circle their valleys in minutes when herdsmen spotted tax collectors approaching. Many of the horses Columbus took to the Americas came from La Gomera.

Atlantis was reputed to lie somewhere on the ocean floor between the Canaries and the Azores.

After a few days of living in the villa, I began to walk down the steep hill to the *piscina*, or swimming pool, on the edge of the little port. There was beach swimming too, but the beach was more gravel than sand. The undertow was severe and often had small boulders whirling in it.

The study of local wildlife was much better at the *piscina*. The girls came in all shapes, some of them spectacular. Puerto de la Cruz had long been an English vacation spot and had many permanent residents of English extraction. The Scandinavians were best represented, and a Swedish girl named Hilavi ran a beach boutique. She later became a Miss Universe. There were Germans, Dutch, Austrians, French, people from almost everywhere except the United States.

For a week, I made book on the local talent. It was not so easy as it is now. The islands were a part of Catholic Spain, and because of that there were no bikinis or bare breasts. The year before, a government minister from Madrid had come holidaying to Puerto Cruz with his family, which included two teenaged daughters. Although none of the bathers or swimmers wore daring suits, something offended him, and he closed the pool and the beach for a week.

Late one afternoon, after visiting the pool, I trudged back up to the villa in darkening light. As I turned into the drive winding down between the tall banana plants, the white house was dark. This was normal because both my servants, Bernarda the cook and Carmen the little maid, had gone home for the day. I usually wrote for a couple of hours at twilight and did not want them underfoot.

This night an addition had been made. When I had walked down the long hall and turned into the glass-walled *sala* I saw a large Christmas tree winking with colored lights, several gifts scattered around its base. A stranger in a strange land, I smiled and knelt beside the tree. Don Enrique, my landlord, had prepared a welcome for Christmas Eve.

Because I had no gifts to buy locally, I had forgotten that the holiday had begun. Among the presents was a bottle of Carlos Primera brandy. I opened it, poured a drink, and bowed toward Don Enrique's house, murmuring, "*Feliz Navidad!*" My thoughtful landlord was the same man who had once run the Nazi flag up on the roof pole over the villa. This was right after the Wehrmacht had engulfed the Ruhr Valley. Outraged residents in the permanent English colony below had retaliated by firing rifles at his huge glass windows.

Then I poured another drink of the fine brandy and lifted it toward my ex-wife and ten-year-old son Shawn, somewhere beyond the Western Ocean.

ONE OF THE MINOR DELIGHTS of lounging in the Elysian Fields was that you could drink champagne for breakfast. The Spanish made a bubbling wine called Codorníu, a distant relative of real champagne but very cheap. German *sekt* is of this type. After casing the local situation, I became a minor dissolute and swordsman. I made a fair target, being tanned, six feet tall, thirtyish, and accompanied by money.

There was a Finnish countess named Prosterus who had a nubile daughter, and I had several impressive *haute cuisine* dinners with her, but the make was too obvious. I went to flower festivals in Orotava, but the Spanish girls all had *duennas*. Many of them were striking beauties, but they were inaccessible. The English girls were wan and not very energetic. Like most long-time residents of small islands, they had become wan from the fever such residence entails.

As usual, the best one eluded me. There was a slender Swede with considerable style and a constant retinue of haughty young dons, sons of the banana millionaires. They were all prouder than God on a good day, for reasons I could not place, and they accompanied her everywhere, to the beach, the *piscina*, the hotel dances, the island excursions. Her name was Kerstin Lil Singbritt Manfreds Arnkloo Hermelin, and she had recently been divorced from Baron Hermelin of Stockholm. Slightly horse-faced in a patrician way, she smiled at me as mockingly as a Giaconda. No, she was unable to have dinner with me. Sorry. She danced as lightly as a prima ballerina and seemed to view the human race with mild amusement. She had an older sister, Caisa Britta, a tall blonde with two children by a rich alcoholic American. I thought that might be why the ex-baroness refused my simplest requests.

Several months after I had moved into the villa, I flew back to the States, sold my house in Fort Worth to my older brother Edwin, and visited my ex-wife and son in Fort Lauderdale, Florida. After a New York trip to see my agent, I bought a small English car and drove it to Houston. After booking passage to Tenerife on a freighter, I walked into the music department of Foley's and, in an hour, bought what the salesman swore was their best sound machine, a Zenith Cobramatic. To go with it I bought almost every jazz and blues album on display—Billy May, Ellington, Sinatra, King Cole, Eartha Kitt, Garland, Fitzgerald, and the strings of Mantovani.

When I boarded the freighter, I had what looked like a cardboard baby's coffin under one arm. A Tenerife pediatrician named Gil Mendez Bencomo had asked me to pick it up in New York. It was an X-ray tube he had been trying to get for two years. I had immediately smelled a small rat, but Gil, a fine doctor, had assured me that the tube would fit in my pocket. When the freighter docked in Santa Cruz de Tenerife, Dr. Mendez was waiting, took possession of his big X-ray tube, and got the port authorities to wave my new car and other baggage through without inspection.

The next week was open house in the white villa. I took Trenkel's teenaged daughter riding in the little English car, and the *sala* was crowded with dancing visitors as the Cobramatic's speakers boomed Nat Cole's wails into the Vale of Orotava and down into Puerto Cruz. Almost everybody came.

One night after midnight, the party had broken up and I was cleaning up its debris when the front doorbell jangled. I walked down the dark hall and found her standing there alone.

"Why is it," she inquired, "that every ill-favored slut on the island has been invited to hear your albums, and I have not?"

"Come in, Kerstin Lil," I said. "You're late."

SO BEGAN AN AFFAIR OF SUCH INTENSITY that it dwarfed any I had had previously. Sexually, we were like two snakes gliding in a pond. There were no constraints. Kerstin Lil did not come to me as a vestal virgin, nor I to her as a deacon of the church. No rules existed, no shibboleths, and no appointments to keep. I seemed at last to be free of the false premises of the country-club society I had arisen from.

Slowly, I began to learn from her. We held what was almost a continuous open house in the cliffside villa, and during one of these impromptu galas, I taunted a young American boy who was obviously gay. Kerstin Lil interrupted my baiting by leading me into the kitchen. "You are not allowed to pick on Rikki," she said. "He is a guest in your house. You will treat him with a courtesy that fact implies." I started to interrupt, but she angrily waved me to silence. "I know you're a hotshot writer with your name in big American magazines, propping up the Kotex ads, but you are the host here. You are not allowed to act like a big fool!"

As the months ran on under sun-flooded skies, I began to miss Kerstin Lil during the brief periods when she was not with me. I suggested that she move into the villa, where she could have the master bedroom and the adjoining smaller one for Lou, her black-eyed four-year-old daughter. The huge connecting bathroom had two bidets. Lil said she could not do that: Baron Hermelin, Lou's father, might try to use such residence to claim custody of the child. That made sense, but I brooded on it for a while longer, then suggested that if we were married, Lou's father could have no objection. Lil said she would consult her parents, who lived in Lund, Sweden.

When they agreed to the union, Lil flew to Stockholm to prepare for the nuptials, a simple private civil ceremony. I was to follow her to Sweden.

My first indication that we were not dealing with just a second marriage came in a letter from my lawyer brother Olcott in Fort

Worth. He said that private detectives had been interrogating a number of Texas sources about my past and that he had received a letter from a major Stockholm law firm with certain demands. The first and most formidable was that he furnish, on my behalf, affidavits from every judicial system in the United States, warranting that I was in fact legally divorced and able to assume another union in Sweden. Olcott had explained to the Stockholm firm that such affidavits were not possible and that my bill of divorce in Tarrant County, Texas, would suffice.

All of a sudden, my little insular romance in the Canaries was becoming complicated. Kerstin Lil was an attractive and intelligent lady I had met on the beach. My attempt at a merger was revealing a hidden infrastructure with corporate outlines.

When notified, I flew to Kastrup Airport in Copenhagen and checked into the Hotel d'Angleterre. Lil took the ferry over from Malmö and we began to rehearse for the approaching nuptials.

AFTER I HAD CHECKED INTO THE D'ANGLETERRE, before Kerstin Lil joined me, I had a chat with the hotel manager on duty, then went around to the offices of Copenhagen's largest newspaper. There, the press card I had used on a previous European trip got me into their files.

Manfred Arnkloo, Lil's father, was a heavyweight in Sweden. His bio said that he had come from a Skane farming family and had worked as a drayman in his boyhood. After rising to village-level affluence, he had become the first Ford dealer in Sweden. Later he switched to General Motors and had agencies in several cities. His home was in Lund, and he operated a large racing stable. His horses had won umpty-ump races.

After Lil arrived, we went to see the Little Mermaid statue in the harbor, toured the Tivoli Gardens, and ate at the Seven Sisters restaurant. One night we toured the Nyhavn dock district with a police escort. This area ranked second only to the Marseilles harbor piers in violence, and police always patrolled it in pairs or quartets.

In Lund, I was checked into a small hotel and met Director Arnkloo in his modest home. He was a handsome old man with a big head, bald except for a few strands of hair which he wore woven into a plait. His white-haired wife, who had obviously once been beautiful, bustled about as solicitously as the average mother. We had bean-soup dinner, a weekly ritual. Before the meal was concluded, Director Arnkloo was called to the phone and did not return for some time. Lil told me the call was from his head groom, telling him about race results.

She and I were married in a Stockholm registry office. After spending a week in the capital, during which I had admired the huge statue of Charles XII, his warning metal gauntlet perpetually pointing toward Russia, we went to the Dalarna lake district. By this time I was growing accustomed to Swedish signs and speech.

Following his divorce from Joyce Clayton, Jim Phillips wandered his way to the Canary Islands, where he met and ultimately married expatriate beauty Kerstin Arnkloo, the former Baroness Hermelin of Sweden. *(Author Collection)*

Once in a hangover languor, I had gone to sleep in a barber's chair and awakened with hair curly as Shirley Temple's. At the end of the hotel corridors there was usually a sign which said UPFART. I always tried to oblige. Everybody in Sweden, in response to everything, constantly kept repeating "tak" or "taks a milky." The whole country seemed obsessed, always either with farting or chattering like a clock factory.

Dalarna was a beautiful lake. We had a huge pink porcelain stove in our bedroom. Outdoors, at the *polkagriser*, or peppermint festival, children were dancing in red-and-white-striped costumes complete with candy canes. Finally, we caught a ship of the Salen line in Goteborg for passage back to the Canaries. Our welcoming committee aboard the ship was impressive. It included not only the captain of the vessel but Mr. Salen, the owner of the line.

FOR SEVERAL YEARS MY MARRIAGE to Kerstin continued in Spanish islands and spas. We became a part of that sad cavalcade of expatriates who have enough income to live without working and spend their time pretending to be artists. Mostly they are counterfeits who drift from one pretension to the next, from one hangover to the next, one tropic background to the next. Like Micawber, they all believe something will turn up for them, but their only immediate concerns are unobstructed bowels and unrestricted genitalia.

They exhibit the dramatic excess of the true artist but never manage his production, and deride the world which keeps on being mundane in spite of their informed protests. My time with Kerstin unreeled on Tenerife Island in the Canaries, Barcelona on the Spanish mainland, and two of its satellite spa towns, Sitges and Lloret de Mar. I could feel the trap closing. I made several flights back to the States on real or fancied grounds.

It was an interesting time. We met scores of painters, writers, sculptors, and even critics, but unfortunately no Picasso showed up. Tenerife was a spectacular background for sybaritic living. Barcelona is the queen city of the world, and has everything that implies, including genuine artists. Lloret de Mar, forty-five miles north, was a small place of no distinction, and Sitges was an old foreign enclave down the coast.

For sexual ease and creature comfort, you could not fault this life. But there was a flaw in it that grew larger and larger. I could not write. Our expenses were modest. We rented housing, and daughter Lou's Swedish nanny was paid by Kerstin. In the previous five years, I had published three novels and thirty stories, serials, and articles in leading American magazines. Then the flow from my typewriter stopped abruptly. There seemed no way I could adapt European backgrounds into saleable prose. I even tried imitation Hemingway, but most of that was still being done by Hemingway, and I couldn't master it.

Kerstin had plenty of money, but I did not intend to use it. If I had been working well, the question would never have come up. She never put a foot wrong, and went to absurd lengths to create work spaces to which I could accommodate. She fixed up studios with external stairways, even removed herself and the child from my vicinity when she thought it might help.

Mitchum went to Paris to make a picture, and I flew up to see him. Later, after the picture was shot, he and Dorothy flew to Barcelona and visited Sitges. We continued to outline the idea for his personal production of a film based on the moonshine drivers in the Big Smoky Mountains. It was as yet untitled but became *Thunder Road*.

Getaway day came when Zen cabled me from Fort Lauderdale that Shawn was in difficulty. The school said he needed psychiatric help.

FORT LAUDERDALE WAS DEPRESSING. Zen lived in a rented house with the usual ratty rattan furnishings, and she herself didn't look much better. When we had lived in New York, she had been an authentic beauty, tall, green-eyed, and graceful. One of her jobs in this period had been with five other showgirl-type models in a show in the Persian Room of the Plaza Hotel, and between performances we had wandered in Central Park. Now she had diminished. Gauntness was pulling her out of shape. As one writer had put it, the sevens were up and the elevens were out. Shawn seemed normal enough, and I spent only one night with them before flying on to California. I did not want to know what was hidden in her cheap resort furniture, what was pulling her out of shape.

At the airport she kissed me goodbye, and I hugged Shawn. Zen said that I was the seeker, and that she had often wondered what it was I looked for. "Trying to find the Whizzard, I guess," I told them, and Shawn laughed and clapped his hands. When he was only five, he had searched the neighborhood, looking for the Whizzard.

MITCHUM HAD RENTED AN APARTMENT for me in Westwood, a neighborhood just west of Beverly Hills, and we continued preliminary work on the untitled movie. He was appearing almost constantly in a string of RKO quickies, with Howard Hughes playing remote-control God from Las Vegas. Nothing could be done without his consent, and he could not be contacted directly. You simply filed your request and waited by your phone. Hughes might call after midnight.

Mostly he didn't. Protected by his Mormon zealots, he sometimes launched nonsensical ukases like thunderbolts. I was under contract to the studio for a while. This was because Jane Russell wanted to be more than a pair of publicized breasts, and forced the studio to hire me in the hope I might turn out something that showed her as something more than a phallic symbol. I tried, on an oil field story, where I thought her robust beauty might be shown to best advantage. No dice. We sent drafts to Vegas, and they came back with ways to engineer more enticing brassieres. I concluded that Howard Hughes, whom I much admired as a pilot, was nutty as a fruitcake and sexually immature. In the fourth-draft screenplay I was doing, Jane was wandering into a ranch kitchen where a Chinese cook tries to grope her. I amended it to read that she disposes of his evil advance by stunning him with a baseball bat. Then I caught a plane to Fort Worth. I don't think anybody noticed my departure or the changed ending.

ON THE DARK SIDE OF HIS FORTIETH BIRTHDAY, in 1955, the golden boy was tightening up, edging into shadows. The literary hope of Fort Worth society had become a prolific producer of commercial pablum, a traveling iconoclast, a genius *manqué*. As proof of the constraints, I was attending my first funeral.

Zen, my first wife, was the honoree. She lay, safe now, in the ornate coffin while unctuous ritual phrases poured over it. Beside me, watching from the first row, was our only child. Shawn was fifteen, getting tall, released for the occasion from the high-priced school for problem boys in Arizona.

After it was over and everybody had murmured the proper condolences, I took Shawn to dinner. The boy started to cry and said he couldn't stand the ranch school much longer. I promised him that as soon as the Mitchum movie was in the can, we could go to Tahiti. Shawn had a history of refusing education and running away. He had been booted out of a couple of Episcopal schools, gone missing, and then had been found wandering in the woods.

Zen's death had been sudden but not unexpected. She had phoned the Westwood apartment a couple of times but I couldn't understand what she was trying to say. A few nights later I got a call from Bernice, the maid who had worked for us in Fort Worth and was still with Zen. She was frightened, and I had told her to check Zen into the local hospital and notify her doctor father in Fort Worth.

She died in her father's house a few days later, aged thirty-eight.

I FLEW TO WASHINGTON, DC, to meet Mitchum and went with him to see the head of the Alcohol and Tobacco Tax Unit at the Treasury Department. He was cordial and, because of Mitchum's presence, agreeable. His unit would allow me to withdraw for appraisal the files on all closed cases relating to chase and arrest of illegal alcohol producers in the Big Smokies region. We would have no access to pending cases.

Robert Mitchum does not go to parties. He creates them by sitting still and chatting with people. Early in our friendship, I had learned to avoid being with him in public whenever possible. John Wayne attracted cowboys, polo players, and socialites. Mitch was a magnet for the discontented, minor felons, and sneaky pot gaspers. All the dispossessed and unruly characters seemed to find in him their own window on the world.

I did go with him to have lunch at the Congressional cafeteria. Our host was Representative Joe Kilgore, from the Rio Grande valley, whom I had known in the waning days of War Two as a decorated light colonel in the Air Force. He would later become an eminence in Texas Democratic politics. We had bean soup, which was excellent.

Over the weekend in the Hilton suite, things got intoxicated. I only remember a pleasant haze, spent mostly with a lovely peasant girl who had appeared as if by osmosis. She would, she swore, overwhelm me with her favors if I would put her through beauty school. I awakened Sunday morning wearing her brassiere as an eye patch. Such revelry was not unusual in a Mitchum caravan. Once, in a French Quarter ramble in New Orleans, he had returned from a trawling expedition with a 250-pound nymph carrying her own bicycle.

Sunday night he flew back to California to resume filming while I stayed in the hotel to turn out a treatment on the moonshiner idea. I had already researched the North Carolina-Bloody Harlan County area, the ballads of Elizabethan origin still sung there, the general flavor of chinquapin country, the funerary legend of the whippoorwill, and the cautionary phrases about Jack o' Diamonds.

In two weeks, I had a sixty-page treatment, slugged it *Thunder Road,* and mailed it to Mitchum. The original intent was to make it with another actor in the lead as the first production of DRM, the personal company of Dorothy and Robert Mitchum. Elvis Presley seemed a natural candidate, so Mitch and I went to see him at the Bel-Air Hotel.

Elvis was not far into his screen career. He was a handsome, polite boy, lounging with his entourage of Memphis redneck freaks around the pool table, the principal adornment of his suite. He was wearing a white lace shirt. Even when he was sitting, listening to our spiel, his right leg was jumping visibly. He kept one hand on it.

He had just been notified of his impending draft and somehow knew I had been a Marine sergeant. He asked me how a so-called hotshot like himself would be treated by the troops. I laughed at his concern.

"Man," I said, "you were a truck driver long before you were a boudoir idol. If anybody pops off, just belt him across the chops once. It's that simple."

He nodded, seeming relieved. While the negotiations were going on, he came to a lawn party Dorothy Mitchum gave and was the soberest and politest boy there. His appearance in *Thunder Road* had no chance because Colonel Tom Parker, his mentor, wanted $500,000 and 10 percent of the total gross, at a time when such figures were an absurdity.

The picture was financed by United Artists once Mitchum agreed to star in it himself. After another swing by station wagon through the Big Smoky country, scouting locations from Virginia down through Kentucky, Tennessee, and North Carolina, we chose Asheville as headquarters, and I went to work on the screenplay.

In preparing for *Thunder Road,* we sometimes stumbled inadvertently over enchanted moments. Once, in a Mark Hopkins suite in San Francisco, Mitchum called Keely Smith in Lake Tahoe. She was bandleader Louis Prima's wife, and the featured vocalist at Harrah's. Mitch wanted her for the feminine lead in the whiskey-runner story. She flew down to meet us. There was a piano in the suite, and Keely, almost casually, sang "Autumn Leaves" and "I Wish You Love." There was no applause. It would have been superfluous. We all sat staring into personal memories in the quiet suite, with the noises of San Francisco outside.

Later in that same suite, the usual bawdy crowd of camp followers developed, and some of them opened a sizeable marijuana cache in the master bathroom. When the smell began to approximate a burning rubber factory, I flushed the remaining weed down the toilet. There were indignant faces and threats of harm until I explained to the dumb bastards that Mitchum had already been the victim of the most celebrated pot bust in history, and that our fledgling production would not be helped by another one in a major San Francisco hotel.

That same night Mitch wandered by and suggested we duck the roistering peasants to eat somewhere. I agreed. In an unused bedroom, we phoned the Blue Fox restaurant, but since it was nine o'clock Saturday night, we were told that a reservation was impossible. I assured Mitch that there were a lot of other classy joints in town, but he was at that certain stage of the vodka tide and had made up his mind. "Frank owns a piece of that joint," he said. He called Sinatra in Palm Springs and was told to wait forty minutes and proceed to the Blue Fox. We did, and got a good table and a memorable meal, protected by a phalanx of waiters and maitres de.

ON THE THIRD AFTERNOON after my return to Los Angeles, I was sunning beside the Beverly Hills Hotel swimming pool. Or perhaps swanning is the proper term. Who am I to fight the ambience? While I was watching the shapely lasses undulate before their gimlet-eyed keepers, I heard myself being paged. That was deeply satisfying because I had not arranged the call. It was from J.L., a writer I had met on the RKO lot while walking to a sound stage with Mitchum.

He had mentioned then that he would like to talk to me, and I had said sure. Now, on the phone, he wanted me to come out to his house in Van Nuys. He started giving me directions, but I said I would be there soon, if they didn't move the town while I was on the way. When the valet brought my little rental car around to the front of the hotel, it looked brave, but inferior among the Rollses and Bentleys.

I didn't know much about J.L. He was a tall, diffident man with good manners, one of the highest-paid screenwriters in town, and personal assistant to the most flamboyant studio head. He had been an eastern journalist and had written several novels and a failed play. In the trade publications, I had seen several mentions of the fact that he was doing pre-production on a film about the 101st Airborne.

I got lost twice on the way to Van Nuys, but as long as the streets are fringed with service stations a persistent man is never really lost. J.L.'s house was big but not manorial, centered in its own landscaped acre. Today, it would probably sell for no more than eight hundred thousand dollars.

As soon as I switched off the ignition, the writer came out to greet me. On the way back to his study, I was introduced to his wife, a striking brunette with a lot of history in her face, much of it adverse. She was wearing a deceptively simple-looking dirndl outfit and was on her way somewhere. J.L.'s study was really a library, and the books in it looked used.

How would I like to do a draft on the paratroop war story, based on the treatment they had produced? I said it sounded interesting but I couldn't make a firm commitment until I knew where Mitchum's company was going with the moonshine driver story, although I might be able to handle the paratrooper screenplay if the time allowed. I had enough general background on the subject to fake what I didn't know. We chatted on, spacing our conversation with shots of neat rye. He was a well-informed man in almost every field we touched on, and his sidebar remarks were wry and quick. For two hours, sprawled in the civilized room, we exchanged views and memories, and I watched him fall apart.

He drank like a man on his way to an execution, through the usual phases from boasting—he rattled off strings of pictures he had worked on, most of which I had not seen—to anger and defiance and finally to maudlin self-pity. I was loaded too, of course, but I was only the spectator. He was carrying the emotional load.

I could sort out what was goading him. My presence in our little kabuki was only as the young talent who had not yet defaced as many pages as he had, hadn't made all the impressive dollars, and was a decade behind him in my process of deterioration.

Finally he stood up, swaying and holding to the top of his impressive desk. "I've been here seventeen years, kid. A hod carrier toting shit for . . . for . . . Seventh Avenue mentalities. Know what I've got to show for it?"

I shook my head.

"C'mon." He lurched out of the den, down a hallway, through an enormous kitchen, and across the lawn to a small pen surrounded by a wire fence beside the four-car garage. He stumbled to the pen and pointed.

I leaned over to peer into the pen. There was an animal the size of a dog in the shadows of the big kennel, regarding us with mild interest.

"A sheep!" shouted the famous Hollywood writer. There was a leaf rake leaning against the garage wall. He grabbed it and began rousting the recumbent animal to its feet. It was too big to be a lamb, unhorned, and mud-caked. I guessed that it was a middle-aged ewe. "That's it!" he cried. "After seventeen years at enormous wages, what I got left is *one fucking sheep*."

I helped him back to the house. He was mostly bones in a sack. But when he neared the study again, his drooping head came up. He lunged out of my grasp, homed in on the bar, poured a water glass half full of rye, slopping more of it on the bar surface, and downed the drink. It was the one that made the big difference. Sighing, he slid gracefully to the floor.

That left me in another quandary. What was I supposed to do with the passed-out bastard? I was meditating on this problem when a car crunched up the driveway and went around to the garage. His wife, the poised woman with the troubled face, took one look at him, shook hands, and thanked me for coming. As I left, she was looking down at his motionless figure.

Driving the rental car back to the hotel, I decided that settling down in the movie industry might not be a smart thing to do.

AS BACKGROUND FOR FILMING our story of the reckless mountain boys who drive carloads of whiskey to market, we had chosen Asheville, North Carolina. This pleasant, storied city is situated in a natural gap of the Appalachian Mountains at 2200 feet above sea level. It was the home of Thomas Wolfe and had long been a stylish playground resort for the rich.

When a properly prepared company begins shooting, the housing, logistic, and location arrangements allow orderly progression. Because ours was a new production company, this had not been done. Someone, usually the producer but sometimes the director, will have foreseen problems and removed or nullified them. My words and title had been reduced to paper, but I was only an intelligent possibility, with no experience in principal photography.

All we had was Robert Mitchum and the Big Smoky Mountains. We got a picture made with an undistinguished cast because of his patience and perseverance. Most films, unless you've got a Hitchcock, a David Lean, or a John Ford, are planned disasters out of which you salvage what you can and hope it is impressive, or entertaining.

The first outside telephone call, in Asheville's Battery Park Hotel, was a banshee wail from a woman who said she was Thomas Wolfe's sister but that she had cancer. I couldn't tell exactly what she had in mind. Perhaps she intended to give it to me. It turned out that my presence was essential at a memorial ceremony for Tom Wolfe. Since he had been dead for quite a while, I had his sister call our director, who had researched his life. Another call said that some local malcontents were hooking up our museum-quality copperpot still and its worm to actually begin making white whiskey. The beautiful still had been seized on a raid by revenue agents in the area, and the Treasury Department was allowing us to use it in the film. After that, it was to go on exhibit at the Smithsonian. Knowing that the Alcohol and Tobacco Unit would view this private use unfavorably, I had a guard mounted on the still.

Among our first location shots was one featuring Mitchum and some of the heavies conferring inside a tobacco-curing barn. Since we had no natural light, we had to assemble big-battery kliegs. The scene went well, but immediately after we shipped the film, the owner of the barn showed up with a shocker of a damage bill. He claimed that our intense lights had burned his prime tobacco to snuff.

Another unplanned pleasure was a night when Richard Condon dropped by. He had not yet become the famous author but was a working flack for United Artists, whose money we were spending. When under a full head of high-proof steam, Condon was a better group than the Ritz Brothers.

Bob [Robert] Porterfield, founding father of the Abingdon Theatre in Virginia, dropped by to do a cameo, and we also used Mitchell Ryan and Peter Breck from regional theaters. An assistant production manager, observing that we were not the most cohesive unit in operation, tried to panic the production to see if he could

Shot on a shoestring and lacking all the hallmarks of highbrow cinema, Thunder Road bombed with the critics but won over audiences and is now considered a legitimate 'cult classic.' *(Free Use/Public Domain)*

salvage some loot from the wreckage. Mitchum groaned, finished his drink, and put the conniver on the next train out.

So a picture got made. *Thunder Road* would have been a much better movie if I had been sharper in translating ideas to visual form, but it still was seminal in that it began the closer look at the drivers and lifestyles along those mountain roads. Not until 1969 and *Easy Rider,* would the myth come into sharp focus.

WHILE BROWSING THROUGH the newspapers, I lingered over a short filler story on a man in Kansas City who had been sentenced to fifteen months of psychiatric treatment. His courtship techniques had been bolstered by claims that he was the recipient of two Medals of Honor for rescuing hundreds of prisoners in Viet Nam, and that he was a trysting companion of Elvis Presley and a former high CIA official with the hidden rank of Major General.

Americans have claimed many accomplishments, but the most remarkable of these has never been properly honored. Since the beginning of this country we have produced a singular breed called the bullshit artist. Compared with the best of these, Munchausen was a piker.

Our most recent eminence in this regard is Ollie North. Wandering almost by chance into the upper echelons of national security, this light colonel of Marines found his superiors so busy covering their own asses that the obvious intent of our simpleton President was being ignored. Not by Ollie. Lying as fast as he could speak, winging around the world, he assembled millions of dollars, bought illegal arms, and single-handedly became American foreign policy. In due course, he was tried and convicted for ignoring our laws and the will of Congress, but he has emerged unrepentant as a rich felon. An admirable example of the bullshit artist gone upscale.

North is not, however, the most adroit exemplar of this art. That would be Robert Mitchum. The actor's finest hours have never been before the cameras, although he has spent a lifetime at that. In his dressing room, or in trailers on location, Mitchum effortlessly creates seminars on the great mysteries of life. He does not enlist a coterie. Compatible groups automatically assemble around him.

Mitchum claims to have played everything from a Polish pygmy to a Lebanese whore, but his finest role remains the master of the revels. The Blackfoot guru with the big shoulders is not so much a raconteur as a connection to imagined wonders. In US and European locations, I have heard at least three versions of his escape long ago from a Georgia chain gang, and marveled with other acolytes at his dread band of dognappers. Truth is never a hindrance to Mitchum. He would climb a tree to tell a lie.

In Australia, the aborigines have the dreamtime. Peasants in Mexico gnaw on mushrooms or peyote buds and zoom to the moon. Old men in China inhale poppy smoke and drowse. In Yemen, almost everyone chews the kat leaf to unveil mysteries. Mitchum, meditating in a vodka haze, is a whole new nirvana.

Only once did I break the gossamer fabric of his mantra. We had lunched on bean soup in a Congressional restaurant, and afterward the usual crowd had settled around him in the Washington hotel suite. I forget what saga he was intoning, but the second time he put a geographic tag to it, I interrupted. "Bullshit. There's no town in Louisiana named Penelope's Crotch."

Mitchum's big shaggy head turned toward me briefly. The artist is often plagued by unbelievers. "You could look it up," he said. "There's a post office there."

Next day, squinting through a roaring hangover, I checked my atlas and found to my satisfaction that there was no habitation in Louisiana named Penelope's Crotch. It had been only another genie in the Mitchum bottle.

Still, as I worked at a master scene, trying to make it come to life, I thought what a wonderful throwaway line it would make.

"What you have been doing lately?"

"Oh . . . spent the summer in Penelope's Crotch . . ."

I DON'T KNOW HOW MANY SHIPS on the high seas in 1958 had fools aboard, but I can pinpoint the ship with the biggest fool on it. It was the S.S. *Alameda* out of San Francisco, Matson line, bound for Tahiti. The fool was taking his son to have a look at the fabled island, as he had promised.

Shawn adapted to the Polynesian culture as readily as he had to Mexico. He went shopping with Maeva, the cook, and met her extended family. Both of them put the moves on me until I rented him a motor scooter, after which I sat on the terrace and watched him putt-putt by the bungalow with a succession of nubile beauties perched behind him, riding pillion. The remainder of his time he spent sporting in the water off the beach before the house. He soon demonstrated to me how to swamp a small outrigger canoe, and then how to bail it out again deftly.

Old Dad was not forgotten. At twilight one evening, a stylish lady from the golfing country of Pennsylvania turned into our drive and hailed me on the terrace. We had a few drinks at Quinn's Bar and took a late swim in the secluded waterfall-pool, which I later discovered was the main water supply for Papeete, strictly verboten for recreational purposes. The lady was, as they say in rodeo country, a trifle squirrelly in the hocks, and a dead-game erotic competitor. I suppose she had to be, facing comparison with the dusky native damsels. I heard in the market that she had once had a liaison with Sterling Hayden, the sailor-actor.

Serendipity had smiled on us. After we had gotten off the Alameda and checked into a hotel, I asked about leasing a house. I saw several which were too large and overpriced, and was beginning to think it was a major problem, when a friendly gendarme advised me to go see a certain Chinese merchant. And so, as I had done in buying station wagons for the Burmese charter operation, I walked into a nondescript emporium, explained my requirement to someone

Chinese, and emerged with the best bungalow in Punaauia, complete with Escoffier-type cook.

The pleasant days ran together. A minor mystery appeared and then was forgotten when I did not pursue it. The cook's sister, also Polynesian, worked for a retired film director who lived in an exclusive and well-guarded enclave of huts. All the activities of this group seemed to center around a small American boy. Even if he was only playing with other children, the entry of any adult automatically triggered an influx of armed guards from the shadows of surrounding palm trees. They were always waiting there. I later heard that the object of their constant regard was the illegitimate son of an enormously rich American banker bearing a famous name.

With neither plans nor prospects, I drifted through Tahitian life as I had done in the fringe spas of the Mediterranean littoral. I was drinking heavily, but with Maeva supervising the boy, life moved on without incident. Raymond Chandler, in his last phone call to me in the States, said he would be making Papeete on board a P&O cruise ship in June, and I looked forward to meeting him. Then, in a lucid moment at breakfast, I read in a French newspaper that he had died in London. I had another drink.

One afternoon, a gendarme came up the bungalow stairway with a note from the police commissioner in Papeete. I had met him at a cocktail party aboard a French cruiser, given in honor of a naval officer who was a lineal descendant of Jules Verne. The police chief was a slender, quiet man with a small mustache. As I sat before his desk, he asked casually how I was enjoying my vacation in the Society Islands. I said they were close to Nirvana, wondering what his pitch was. Out the window, in the courtyard to his office, I could see a large rat trying to circumvent a circular tin shield placed around a sloping palm tree.

The commissioner then said that one of his principal jobs was to observe all casual visitors to Tahiti. Because of its idyllic reputation and its permissive and beautiful women, many visitors found it easy to give up entirely. Some of them became public charges. The policeman added that his office had received a dossier on me from its headquarters in Paris, and they were appreciative of the fact that I had been published in several languages.

"But," he added, "I think you would be unwise to apply for a renewal of your visitor's visa."

I was angered. I had funds on the island and more in a Texas bank. When I mentioned this, he nodded agreeably, adding that the boy seemed well cared for and healthy. But, as he pointed out, I was not working and had not been for several months. Mostly I had been drinking.

By this time I was enraged, and asked if a provincial officer held the right to interdiction over all foreign visitors. The police commissioner nodded politely. "Your permit will be up in ten days. It will not be renewed. If you are not on a plane or ship before it lapses, I will officially expel you from French Oceania. That way we would furnish the passage out, but I do not think you will enjoy the accommodations."

WHEN THE NEXT SCHEDULED Messageries Maritimes cruise-liner left Tahiti for Marseilles, Shawn and I were on it. We were the only passengers unloaded in the Panama Canal Zone. We flew from there to New Orleans and Texas. My heavy drinking continued, but only at night and under planned controls. I never took a drink in the daytime, and arranged the evenings so that I could put away a quart and have something to eat when I was finished. If such an oxymoron is possible, I was a prim drunk.

As we walked through the New Orleans airport to make flight connections, I saw that the bad-faced people had taken over the world. Everyone we passed, pedestrians and ticket-counters and officials, had visages of maniacal savagery. Shawn, happy and gamboling, did not seem to notice. When I had delivered him to his grandparents' home, I serviced the little car I had taken to the Canary Islands and drove into Mexico.

In Juarez, after eating at the Cadillac Bar, I loaded the rear end of the car with a case of La Herradura tequila, Garci Crespo mineral water, and a crate of limes. I had no defined destination. There was no conflict in choosing highways. For two weeks, sitting hunched behind the wheel, I crossed the stark and exuberantly tropic vistas of my past.

I was not a gringo menace to highway navigation. Driving was for hangover time, and I never had a drink until the car stopped and the sun was down. The only people I talked to were in filling stations, stores, and hotels.

There is a long stretch, nearly ninety miles long and straight, going east from Mexico's Highway One to San Luis Potosi. As I lowered into it after twilight, a mescal-crazed peon leaped out from behind some bushes and slashed at my tires with a glittering machete. I laughed and swerved, giving him room. It seemed a natural occurrence.

In Manzanillo, I stayed in the same hotel Zen and I had been visiting when the call from New York came, about the sale to RKO. Paricutin, the unheralded volcano which had burst from a farmer's field in 1943, had lost the fire in its belly and was now only a bleak charred column. I greeted it with another quart of tequila and drove on.

In San Miguel de Allende, where we had lived for several years, I stared out over the sooty blue mountains of Guanajuato and remembered the tall, enthusiastic boy from Philadelphia. His name was John Fulton Short. He wanted to become a matador and called himself El Cortito, the Short One. For seventy-five dollars, I bought him a calf to kill in the amateur cape-swirling in the local ring. Several years later, when I was living in Sitges, Spain, he had sent me a Christmas card, expertly hand-drawn. He was in the country trying to break in with the big-league toreros, and I hadn't yet heard whether he'd made it or not. The next time I heard his name, a few years later, he had become the first American to ever qualify as a full matador in Spain and was known around the world for his evocative bullfighting scenes, painted in the fresh blood of his kills.

I revisited Fortin de la Flores, where the swimming pool had been filled with gardenias, and Linares, on the highway, where we had sat laughing in the shade, eating tangerines warm from the trees, and Vera Cruz, where the muggy heat was like a blow in the face, and huge moths curvetted in the humid rooms.

Finally, in enormous Mexico City, sinking into the lakebed, I holed up in the Lincoln Hotel, had another case of Herradura sent in, and started some serious drinking. My hegira along the paths Zen and I had followed in the happy days was over.

"You spent the bright coins too fast, too heedlessly, old sport," I admonished myself. "And even when the nice Swedish lady wanted to help you, you blew that one, too."

The day was over. It was all night.

I WAS IN A CLOSED SOCIETY, separated from the civilian population by locked doors. From my corner of the ward, I watched the four white-clad orderlies converging on Henry B. They moved toward him with expressionless faces, repeating a maneuver they went through several times a week. Henry had been interrupting projects in the occupational therapy room, throwing paints, crayons, and modeling clay around and harassing patients using them.

He retreated to the television room, eyes switching rapidly as the orderlies closed in. He went down shouting and fighting as they bore him to the floor, fitted him into the straitjacket, and deftly jabbed the point of a hypodermic syringe into his thigh. Then they stood gossiping while he relaxed. When the gurney was rolled in, I knew he was bound for the soft room, padded walls and only a mattress for furniture.

I went back to work on my own occupational therapy project, a round copper ashtray into which I was inscribing a significant motif. When I had it completed, I would carefully load it with the requisite powdered colors and bake it in the ceramic oven.

I was forty-four years old and locked up crazy in a psychiatric ward. Destiny's tot had come down in the world. My rap sheet held the diagnosis: Nembutal addiction of long standing. I was behind bars in the shooting gallery of Fort Worth's United States Public Health Service hospital [aka the Fort Worth Narcotic Farm]. There were only two Federal treatment centers for addiction, the other one being in Lexington, Kentucky.

There were thirty-seven of us in the ward. Many, like myself, had signed themselves in, but once the gate closed, it would not open again for ninety days.

We had no keys, matches, belts, or shoestrings. Safety razors were doled out at the service desk, and their use was supervised. Most of us were on a methadone regimen, issued and taken under observation, meant to replace the particular devil which had deranged us.

Barbiturate withdrawal is tricky, because most times it involves epileptiform seizures. The doctor treating me was openly skeptical of the dosage level I had achieved before turning myself in. He said that such Nembutal jolts were in the literature as often causing death. I asked why he did not try me on a dose at the level I had claimed. He did, and checked on me frequently after I had ingested the jumbo load.

I explained to him that I had never in my life taken a Nembutal capsule except for one reason. In a pressure business, I had used the barbiturate as an Off switch to get to sleep. I told him that I had traveled internationally with a large wholesaler's jar containing four thousand grain-and-a-half yellow capsules, which had never been challenged in customs passage.

He shook his head in disbelief. Tracing my dependency on my hammer-like treatment for insomnia, I explained how the addiction had finally begun to rule my waking hours. Several times, in New York, Europe, and California, I had refused invitations to stay overnight in private homes because it would temporarily separate me from my Nembutal stash. I had no hope of even five minutes of sleep unless my mental activity was blacked out by the capsules.

I don't think the doctor fully believed my story, but his interest mounted because I represented a possible article for a medical journal. Doctors love those prospects more than they love specific remedies. This one asked what I would do if I could shake the addiction successfully. I assured him I would never touch another sedative, hypnotic, or soporific again. He noted this prediction on his record.

The copper-ceramic ashtray I was making occupied most of my time. I knew it was meant as therapy, but I tried to work my present dilemma into its construction. After consulting the hospital library to get the exterior construction of the eye right, I fanned out four sections under the lower lid, curving out to meet the circular shape of the tray. The first section held a tipped champagne glass, the second a waterfall of red and yellow capsules, the third a tilted woman's breast, and the fourth a gaily striped fish curvetting in tropic waters. The tray baked well, colors bright. I use it still.

The most interesting patient in the shooting gallery was a doctor, a handsome, Nordic blond in his late thirties. Prior to his confinement, he had been chief of surgery in a big veterans' hospital. He was amiable but he never smiled, and spent hours staring out through the bars of the high windows. He was a speed freak, resorting to amphetamines to meet his tremendous surgical load. All the years of his training, his hard-learned skills, had come to an abrupt ending when pressure twitched his scalpel touch at the wrong times. The doctor who was treating me said it was unlikely that he would be released anytime soon, and that when he did escape the ward, he would never be allowed to perform surgery again.

On my third day in the huge mess hall, I watched an elderly patient seated across from me get up and carry his tray routinely toward the exit lane. We were required to scrape the contents of the trays into large metal garbage containers and stack the trays before we marched back to the ward. This man reached the bank of refuse containers, scraped dutifully, and stacked his tray in the proper place. Then he darted to the nearest unloading can and began to scoop up slops from the bottom of it with both hands, jamming dripping garbage into his mouth and over his entire face. He was immediately surrounded by watchful guards and led out of the mess hall. A ward nurse told me that he made this singular dessert rush about once a week. He had been confined in psychiatric wards for thirty-one years, in so many institutions that no one could remember what the initial diagnosis had been.

I had been retrieved from the gloom of the Mexico City hotel suite by my older brother, Eddie. He performed the mission with his usual efficiency but little enthusiasm. As the phrase goes, or should, "He's my brother, and he's goddamned heavy." Eddie was civil but obviously thought I was getting a little old to be collapsing in foreign capitals. He squared accounts at the hotel, and we drove up Highway #1 to Laredo in my little Metropolitan.

After we had crossed the international border and checked into a hotel, he got a call from his wife, scolding him for neglecting his law practice, so he flew back to Fort Worth. In quick succession, I flopped around in Austin and Dallas, still drinking hard and undergoing two epileptiform seizures. Through the pain and fog, I wanted to go home but could not locate that place. When I tried to watch television, fiery comets spiraled out of the screen and fractured my sight. I fell down a flight of stairs, loose as a meaty doll, and broke some ribs. Still out of control, I applied for permission to spend ninety days in the locked ward and was driven to the big federal hospital.

One of the friends I made in the bug ward was a cheerful young burglar with an odd complaint. Not yet twenty, he had been fairly successful at his trade, spending more time out of the joint than in it. On his last forced-entry job, he had gone in through an attic window of a house left empty by vacationers. While crawling through the rafters toward the interior stairway, he had inadvertently raised his head and struck it against an exposed electrical connection. This had fried his scalp, burning the hair off, and left an ugly exposed wound on the top of his head. It had nearly scarred over but left his appearance so grotesque that he always wore a cap or hat. One more trip to surgery, he confided, would so reduce the mound of burned tissue that he could wear a hairpiece or wig and look human again. Remarking that I seemed to know all the big dogs in the hospital, he asked if I couldn't arrange for some bleeding-heart Jesus society to furnish him a wig. I mentioned the case of the worthy felon to some visitors, and they got him the hairpiece. He was delighted and paraded through the ward wearing it at all hours. The trouble was that he looked like a young Wallace Beery in a Shirley Temple toupee.

After I had been in the shooting gallery for sixty days, they turned us all out for a pickup baseball game. I played shortstop, but my performance was so dismal that it saddened me. Once a good infielder with lots of range and a good arm, I found that my kinetic skills were gone. At my age, I could not have been very sharp, but I had no depth perception and stumbled around aimlessly.

A few days before my voluntary ninety-day incarceration period was up, I met the medical staff. They considered my daily reports and were agreed that I had made remarkable progress. The chief doctor said that a report of my case, in light of my past record of publication, would make a contribution to the medical literature on barbiturism. Would I consider staying in the hospital for a longer period? They would provide me a rent-free apartment on the grounds, and no restraint would be placed on my movements on or off the institute. My copper-ceramic ashtray was solemnly exhibited and the doctors nodded approvingly over its composition and coloration.

I thanked the elders for their suggestion but refused it, adding that their treatment had been effective and that in the future I would never again use barbiturate medication in any form or get myself in a situation where I was locked up and somebody else had the key.

I was released from the ward at nine o'clock one September morning and my personal belongings returned. The little Metropolitan had been brought out to the hospital parking lot and my typewriter and clothes were in the back of it. At my request, no member of the family was there, and with forty-six dollars in my pocket, I drove the little car northeast toward an unknown destination. I was on the move again, a person of no fixed abode.

IT DIDN'T BOTHER ME THAT I HAD NO DESTINATION. The little white boy was still searching for the Whizzard. He was over forty now and had stubbed his toe a few times. He had two failed marriages, his only son was being cared for by former in-laws, and he'd been locked up for crazy. These lapses were mortal but no hill for a stepper. He knew the invisible scene-shifters were at work as always, re-staging the world for his entry at a different angle. Hadn't they already whipped him up an impressive Assamese vista framed by tremendous mountain peaks, and a grandstand seat in a Burmese civil revolt? Not to mention the towering ziggurats of Manhattan, the unabashed conspicuous consumption of Hollywood, the fabled tropic isles where the view from his bedroom window was a snow-topped peak, framed by equatorial bananas across the Vale of Orotava. Mischance and his own arrogance had brought him low at forty-four. He was impoverished except for walkabout money, driving toward a new interior stage in his own country and with a complete change of cast.

I stopped in Texarkana to fill the car with gas, which is about all you can do in Texarkana. Up the highway to Fort Smith, where the hanging judge once strung up malefactors from the Indian nations in clusters like bananas. Then a scenic drive up through the Boston Mountains to Fayetteville for an afternoon in the university library, checking old fragments about Eureka Springs, Arkansas, a precipitous hamlet in the northeast part of the state.

At the turn of the century, Eureka Springs had been a famous spa with a population of twenty thousand, where swells arrived on two trains a day from the east and north. The famous cattle rancher John Simpson Chisum had died there of throat cancer after the Lincoln County range war in New Mexico. Carrie Nation had marched through the taverns of the town like a dark angel of righteousness, smashing bottles of demon rum and the pates of protesting bartenders. She was also against corsets and short skirts.

The author's third wife, Martha Louella Phillips, née Tuttle, was a grounding force for Phillips's wanderlust, providing a stable environment for the last twenty years of his life and writings. *(Author Collection)*

The trains didn't run to Eureka Springs anymore, and the population had dwindled to fourteen hundred. The land around its steep contours wouldn't allow farming, and the vaunted springs had been neglected, several of them being contaminated. What was left was a half-hearted attempt at folk music and crafts. In short, not much. I decided to go show them what a real ruin looked like.

On the way, I visited Rogers and genuflected to the Daisy air rifle factory. While swimming at the municipal pool, I noted a tall, attractive brunette in a blue suit. There was no lifeguard but a girl sunbathing near me said her name was Martha. I made a note of it and began driving around the precipitous switchbacks to the northeast, toward the played-out spa which had been called the Little Switzerland of the Ozarks.

THE JOURNEY ENDED WHEN I DROVE my little car down the precipitous main street of Eureka Springs. After checking into the decrepit Basin Park Hotel, I went to the liquor store next door. The proprietor was a reserved man of middle age whose voice did not possess the regional twang. As he put my Cutty Sark in a paper bag, I remarked on it, and he said that he was retired from a major oil company. Since his store had a front-and-center position on the main street of the village, I asked if he knew where I could rent a reasonably clean, small apartment.

Bob Godbold, the proprietor, handed me my change and asked what my business was. I told him I was a writer, dropping in a couple of titles I thought he might recognize. He said to try the woman tending bar in the joint next door. She owned the building and had a small apartment available. I went around to see her and was briskly interrogated in the beerish gloom sparked by the jukebox music and commercial neon symbols.

I had a look. The place had a separate entrance and was clean enough, and she was asking fifty dollars a month. I handed her a hundred-dollar check, and she agreed to have the electric meter hooked up the next day.

Upstairs in the old hotel, I chased the Scotch with club soda and ran a mental inventory. I had an income of a few hundred dollars a month, what remained of inherited oil royalties. I had published five novels, a small book of poetry, and more than fifty short stories, most of them in the major markets, including several serials. But I had never had a big book commercially, and I had never attended a writer's conference or engaged in correspondence with other writers. I had made several trips to Hollywood and taken some money out of the place, but *Thunder Road* with Mitchum was the only picture I had ever taken all the way through. I had never pursued my brief acquaintance with the few stars I had known, and when Wayne's office had found me during the Mexican drunk to offer me a writing job on his movie *The Horse Soldiers*, I had wired him that I couldn't participate because Warner Color was too brown.

I had been admired by some, but had no friends because I didn't answer mail and refused most telephone calls. Several times, routinely, *Who's Who* had requested me to write an entry in the record of contemporary greatness, but I had not answered. My idea of friendship was when you could send a simple message to the supposed friend saying you were in trouble and needed help, and the party addressed would report to you without delay.

On that basis my older brother, Edwin, would seem to have qualified. He had pulled me out of the Mexico City hotel hideyhole without even being asked. But that one was a phony too. He had extricated me from the high-proof mire, but once he had hauled my troublesome carcass into Laredo, across the international border, he had pulled out, leaving me to flounder in a couple of other towns before the psychiatric ward got me. And when I was locked up there, he had not visited me.

The genesis for these actions had come just before I set out for the Canary Islands. Since two of my brothers were lawyers, they had each handled some of the details involved in my journey. I was riding high at the time, having nearly $90,000 on hand from studio work and a magazine serial. I explained to Edwin that I was profligate and would manage to blow that and more, as I always had. It would be helpful for my future security if he would sell me, at a reasonable price, some of his oil royalty inheritance.

He concurred, and we settled on my purchase of his part of a Hutchinson County interest, which was paying about forty dollars a month. I paid him $4,000 cash and came out with approximately eighty dollars a month income, figuring the matter on a seven-year payout. Several years later, while I was still living in Europe, there was deep drilling on the Hutchinson tract and its income doubled.

Based on a normal life of the pay zone, it appeared that I would be making at least $100,000 extra on the deal.

Edwin suggested that because of this unforeseen increment, we split the profits. When I refused, saying that the Hutchinson selection had been his idea and random, that I had never known anything about any of the royalty properties, his sense of brotherhood was diminished.

Olcott Phillips, the other lawyer brother, was still practicing in Fort Worth and had been of great help in my travels, especially in the Swedish marriage. Because his wife had a private fortune, he was not much hostage to circumstances. David, the younger brother, had owned an English-language newspaper in Santiago, Chile, called *The South Pacific Mail* and was nearing the end of a decade of service as a CIA agent in South America. We had not communicated since he had participated in the overthrow of Jacobo Árbenz in Guatemala back in 1954.

NO BETTER EXCUSE FOR IDLENESS has ever been invented than claiming to be a writer. You can stroll about, drowse at noon, or just stare into the distance. As long as you keep your mouth shut, nothing more is required. If the building collapses around your ears, a bystander is sure to inform the ambulance driver: "He's a writer. He was thinking when it happened."

There was an excellent weekly newspaper in Eureka Springs. I read every word of it, particularly the want ads. Revealing insights into an area's strengths or weaknesses can be found in what a community buys, sells, or discards. Nowhere else had I seen growing ginseng offered for sale. If you answered the ads, you would be directed or led to patches of the wild plant with the aromatic root.

The people who placed these ads belonged to the basic class of society in Eureka Springs. This cleft in the mini-mountains of the Ozarks held the westernmost ebb of the great Anglo-Saxon wave of immigration, which had flooded down through the Big Smokies and left the mountains strewn with Elizabethan ballads and customs. Most of the men still resented intruders and looked like faulty sketches discarded by Giacometti.

These chill-eyed natives of the Ozarks were dissimilar from their redneck shitkicker brethren in the flatter lands below them. Their only real similarity lay in the pickup trucks holding the inevitable rack of hunting rifles in the rear window.

The target of their ads was another class entirely, the lower-class retirees and pensioners from neighboring industrial areas, principally Chicago. They ran the Mom-and-Pop business enterprises and were principally roaring conservatives. Aligned to but not of this group were the would-be artistes, who painted a little or wrote a little or enthusiastically cast the disproportioned ceramic pot. Their bad art was usually turned into bad crafts, which were hawked listlessly to tourists seeking local color.

As I walked and talked and observed the town, these three levels of society came into sharp focus, because there were only fourteen hundred people in the whole village. There was another addition which almost defied definition. When the white immigration wave rolled through Tennessee and the Carolinas, eyeing as always anything valuable it did not yet own, the rich Cherokee tribal lands were an obvious magnet. The proud, intelligent, and progressive tribe obviously had to be uprooted. The Supreme Court ruled that they could not be evicted from their ancestral homelands, so President Andrew Jackson announced that the Court had made their decision, now by God let's see them enforce it! He ordered the army in to disobey the law and evict the Cherokee. Eureka Springs had been on the northern fringe of the Trail of Tears, and remnants of its passage still marked the lunatic expulsion.

While I was having a beer one day, in the bar below my apartment, I asked the owner about poke salad. She said the pokeweed plant grew wild all around the town but its shoots could only be harvested safely for salad greens in the spring. The roots and berries were poisonous, and care had to be taken when preparing the greens.

I thanked her and was outside, getting into my car, when a local boy I had noticed before tapped on my window. I lowered it and greeted him. He said diffidently that if I was interested in poke greens, he could lead me to the best patch of them in Carroll County and cook me up a mess of them.

I said that sounded great. When? Tomorrow, this same time. Meet right here.

The boy had a round face, dark complexion, lanky hair, and a patient, rebellious mule-set to his conical head. He appeared to be the same age as my mid-teen son. The next day I picked him up and he directed me through overgrown timberlands to an abandoned sawmill site. There along the verges of the lane he crouched among the knee-high patches of pokeweed and began plucking a few tender green top shoots from each, putting them in a paper sack.

Again being directed by him, we drove back to Eureka Springs to a small house, almost a shack, on the lower road which led out north to Missouri. The boy, who had introduced himself as Lonnie, got busy in the kitchen part of the one-room structure. He boiled the green shoots twice, then simmered them for a few minutes in clean water with a little vinegar and fatback added.

The little house was almost surgically clean, and I had the feeling that Lonnie did not live alone. There were two makeshift closets with curtains drawn over them. Lonnie put portions of the fragrant greens on two platters, whisked two cold bottles of Jax beer from an ancient refrigerator, and we sat down to our salad entree. It was excellent, and I mopped the last drops of mine up with a piece of bread.

Lonnie was beaming when I left. We shook hands, and I asked if he would take me noodling sometime. Noodling means barehanded underwater fishing. He inclined his head, half-shrugging, as if to indicate "why not?" As I drove up toward the precipitous main street, I was trying to remember where it was Shakespeare had mentioned poke salad.

There had been another presence in the immaculate little shack. Boys or men living solo strewed things around more. After I had made the first upward turn, on impulse, I pulled off into a small overlook from where I had an unobstructed view of the little house I had just left. In a couple of minutes, a bulky figure emerged from the scrub-oak cover behind it and walked to the back door of the shack. I sat a few minutes more but nothing else happened, so I drove on up to the main block and walked to Bob Godbold's liquor store next to the Basin Park Hotel. I was well into acquiring squatter's rights to the seat on top of his cooling cabinet.

When I told him about the trip with Lonnie and the good greens and the strange addition to the shack after my departure, he nodded. "His mother," he said. "She's a blanket squaw, seldom goes anywhere. Remnants of the Tears Trail, I guess. I heard once that their family name was Kanilu, which would put them in pretty fast company." Kanilu had been one of the legendary Cherokee leaders before their forced removal to Oklahoma from the Atlantic coast.

As the faces among the local citizens in the little hill town came into focus, Godbold was the mine from which I got nuggets about their backgrounds. The proprietor of the liquor store was a reticent man ordinarily, an outlander like myself, but he was literate and we developed an affinity of view.

I noticed that he seemed to do considerable business for such a small town, especially in case lots. His reply, after consideration, was that I could only see the tip of the iceberg. Those big orders, repeated at regular intervals, were going deep into the scrubby bush. Major branches of American fascist hatred had gone to ground near Eureka Springs and were buried from sight of the highways. These groups—survivalists, anti-nuclear, anti-Jew, and anti-Black—were in paramilitary-type training camps, located from northeastern Arkansas to and across the Missouri state line. Most had their women and children living with them in secluded encampments, their privacy assured by arsenals of high-tech military weapons. It was to them that the caseloads of liquor and beer were going. "They're the ones you don't see," said Godbold. "They phone the orders in and pick them up in their own trucks. But the town itself picked up a dandy new resident last summer. Gerald L. K. Smith. Ever hear of him?"

"Yes. One of Huey Long's chief henchmen. Delivered his eulogy. Fell out with the movement later. I heard he was in California, publishing something called *The Cross and The Flag*, anti-Semitic bilge."

"The same fellow. Only we've got him now. Family and followers in one of those big wooden castles up Spring Street, complete with stained-glass windows."

"Nobody in the city government protested?"

"No. He's charmed them silly with his saintly money, which he seems to have plenty of. He's seeking tax abatements for a huge new cement statue he intends to erect. A Christ of the Ozarks with outstretched arms. Plans to make it the key piece for an annual passion play, like in Germany."

I shook my head in wonder. "Imagine it. An American blood-brother to that Jew-hater Richard Wagner. I can see how he might get by with it in these hills, but won't anybody in Little Rock have guts enough to scream outrage?"

Godbold surveyed me sorrowfully. "Phillips, you're brand new in these parts. The governor of this state is named Orval Faubus."

For weeks after that, as I watched from my window seat in the liquor store, the brisk, often crewcut paramilitary soldiers of the hidden hate groups took delivery of liquor in case lots. Their presence was unremarked in the street traffic caused by tourists, musical festivals, and folk arts-and-crafts shows. The warriors-in-training never caused trouble, and I wondered when their various jihads against the establishment would begin.

I never saw Gerald L. K. Smith in person, but preparations for his huge Christ of the Ozarks statue were evident. After staying in Eureka Springs for two years, I moved back to Fayetteville and then to St. Louis. Once, I did go back to see the completed statue. It was big enough, but the head was outsized for the body and it had an unbalanced look.

One of the training groups over beyond Harrison became known as the Posse Comitatus. Their contention was that all US currency was fraudulent because of collusion between the Federal

Reserve System and the banks. They held that the Federal Reserve was unconnected to the government but owned entirely by member banks and operated solely for their benefit. About a decade later, most of its leadership died in a burning farmhouse which had been surrounded by a group of heavily armed lawmen.

A larger group, which had hidden training encampments in Arkansas and across the line in Missouri, called itself The Covenant, the Sword, and the Arm of the Lord. Their Lord was entirely white and gentile. A decade after I left Eureka Springs, one of their trainees shot and killed a Missouri state trooper after being stopped by him on the highway. In the ensuing public clamor, most of these hate groups moved out to Nevada or Montana, and later to Washington and Oregon. They robbed several banks to finance operations, and in Denver, executed a Jewish talk-show host named Alan Berg. Soon the FBI and other federal groups were in pursuit, and a significant part of their leadership was surrounded in a house and barbecued while armed authorities watched.

There was less electrifying news. The man who invented Toni hair curlers had built a house near Eureka Springs but was rarely seen. Irene Castle, survivor of the dancing team Irene and Vernon Castle of Broadway and silent film fame, had a house in town and was sometimes seen. The sole hotel of any quality had originally been built by a notorious quack doctor, but he was long since departed. There was still some moonshining done in the hills, but it was of inferior quality, sometimes lethal. The farmers who produced it as a sideline usually used auto radiators as a shortcut and got considerable lead residue in their product. So, of course, I had to tell Godbold about the moonshining picture I had worked on in North Carolina with Robert Mitchum.

Godbold discussed other people's business much more frequently than he did his own. It was not until I had known him for nearly a year that I learned he had two startlingly beautiful grown daughters. As to why he and his poised wife had wound up in Eureka Springs, he deflected the question, saying that after he had retired from the foreign cadre of a big American oil company in Venezuela, the place seemed as good as any.

That was not a typical remark from him. Then one night, just before he was closing the liquor store, he said that while he was in Venezuela, he had been able to get a new-model Oldsmobile shipped in from the States when that was difficult to do. He must have been fairly high in the corporate hierarchy, but when his boss requested the use of the new car over a weekend, Godbold had told him to go screw himself.

That confession cleared things up considerably. His refusal must not have been conducive to promotion in a foreign enclave on the shores of Lake Maracaibo.

IT WAS MIDMORNING, AND I WAS seated alone in the back of the coffee shop, the only customer. The cashier was reading a newspaper, and a faint clatter was coming from the kitchen. A big jovial man came in briskly, followed by three henchmen, and took the circular table in front, overlooking the street. I had seen the big man's face before, in another setting. It was the exact face of a bookmaker at an Irish race course outside Dublin.

His lackeys were providing the incidental airs, light chin music to which he barely listened. They all ordered coffee, interspersing their requests with the usual mindless camaraderie. That was what the table was for, a communal gabble setting.

One of the sycophants, wearing big overalls, came back to my table. "Mr. Teague would like to see you," he said.

I nodded. "Not difficult. Tell Mr. Teague to turn his head and he can see me fine."

That perplexed the messenger. He mumbled, "Well, hell," turned and went back to the front table.

In another minute, the big man was standing before me. "Mornin'," he said.

"And to you too. Sit down."

He did so, moving gracefully for a man who must have weighed two hundred thirty. The waitress brought him a cup of coffee.

"Seen you around," he said. "What do you do?"

"Not a thing. I'm a drunk and a dope fiend, about halfway out of a job."

"Okay. I think you're a bullshit artist. Heard you used to be kinda famous. Writer, worked in New York and Hollywood."

"Are you asking me, Mr. Teague, or telling me?"

"Neither one. I want you to go to work for me, get me reelected."

That got my attention. I thought curiosity had brought him to my table. So I told him that I had done publicity work but had never pushed a candidate in an election. He brushed the thought aside.

"Ain't hard to outwit these peckerwoods. What would you charge to take a shot at it?"

I made a pretense of reading my coffee grounds. "Thousand dollars a week," I said.

He straightened up like someone had jabbed him with a fork. "Jesus H. Christ Almighty God! Man, I'm just running for a representative's seat from a poor Arkansas county, not Chief Justice of the Supreme Court."

"Well." I shook my head. "Looks like I priced myself out of the market."

Teague got up, shaking his head, and commented that the governor of Arkansas only got ten thousand dollars a year. Would I come to see him at four o'clock that afternoon at his office in Berryville so he could explain the problem? I nodded, and he turned back toward the front table.

I went to my own office, which was sitting on the cooler in the front end of the liquor store, and told Godbold that Pat Teague had offered me a job. He said that Teague could afford it. He was a fat cat, with an office-warehouse in Berryville out of which he brokered walnuts, pecans, ginseng to Chinese and Korean markets, fur pelts, and herbs. He owned real estate in Berryville and several farms. He ran a turkey business too. For six years, he had been the Carroll County representative in the Arkansas Legislature, a member of several committees, and Chairman of Agriculture. Godbold added that he didn't think Teague was crooked but had no way to be sure. He was in trouble for only one reason. He would not get out of his Cadillac to shake a voter's hand. Never had. He didn't drink anymore but once had been a carouser.

Berryville is eleven miles from Eureka Springs, a pleasant drive through riverine country. Teague's office in front of the warehouse and loading dock was well-furnished. I was greeted by a pleasant lady who said she was Minna Lee Teague, his wife. She directed me down a stairway to an elaborate underground recreation room featuring a pool table and a huge poker table. The Irishman got up from a sectional sofa to greet me and offered a drink. I declined, sat down, and said I would keep my mouth shut until he had told me the story of his life.

He was originally from Tennessee but had migrated to the Ozarks as a boy. There was no real work available, so he had earned fifty cents a day picking up rocks in hillside pastures. Sometimes helping dynamite stumps in the fields. Gradually, he had built up a brokerage business in national markets. When he had talked himself to millionaire status, I interrupted.

"I'm told that you can't be re-elected because all the citizens ever see of you is the ass-end of your Cadillacs. That in six years you have never addressed any size political gathering, bought any radio time, or attempted to find out in person what your constituents might think or need."

Teague snorted. "Of course I ain't mingled with these brush-apes. I got a bad back from working those fuckin' rocky pastures at half a buck a day. My doctor warned me against riding in a truck or even a pickup."

"Okay. So the Cadillacs are a doctor's prescription. What about the lack of personal contacts, pressing the flesh in person? Not even a salutation on radio?"

The big ruddy-faced man frowned. "Why I'm tryin' to hire you, ain't it?"

I got up and spread the folded tear sheets of newsprint flat on the pool table. They had been hastily drafted for me by Bob Wheeler, the layout and graphics man for the Eureka Springs weekly newspaper owned by his parents. Full pages, bearing top-center a portrait of F. A. "Pat" Teague, and broken hunks of laudatory copy proclaiming him to be the greatest Ozark agricultural asset since the plow, touting his years of service, membership on fourteen House committees, membership on the Legislative council, seniority ranking.

Teague leaned over the pool table, switching on the bright overhead light. He examined the ad layouts and, for the first time since I had met him, smiled. "Like I said," he murmured, "a bullshit artist supreme."

I showed him the smaller layouts for cards and a brochure, all banded in red-white-and-blue, featuring small photos of his phiz.

"Goes like this," I said. "The page ads to run next Sunday, cards and brochures to be distributed the following week. Also a corona-edged poster on heavy print stock, three colors silk-screened, to be tacked on trees and barns anywhere in the county where it ain't illegal. Next week you'll deliver a taped radio speech on the local station here. Not difficult, because you can rehearse it a thousand times. Your voice is bass pitch, fine for recording. You can teach a dog how to record if you're patient."

Teague's face was alive. He could see the victory ahead. He even had a contribution of his own to make, suggesting that he have his hangers-on spread the word around the county that his opponent screwed pigs.

That startled me. "Come again?"

"We'll strew the rumor through every beer joint in the county that the bastard fucks pigs."

"Is it true?"

"Of course not. But we'll force him to deny it publicly."

Politically, it was a basic concept but not new. I told him we wouldn't use it, that we would proceed along the lines I was indicating. That my price, non-negotiable, was $750 a week. He would pay me nothing until election day, and only then if he won.

He mulled that over, nodded, and we shook hands on it.

BY NOW I WAS BECOMING MORE of a player than a spectator in the Ozark follies. On the other hand, I was getting very little liver for my cat, and wondered if the tall brunette I remembered from the Rogers swimming pool really did have legs that long, and how spirited the defense to their cleft might be. I called her on the phone, which was not difficult. She was a night telephone operator.

We went swimming the next afternoon, and I admired her symmetry again. She had the next night off, so we arranged an al fresco revel in the hidden meadow along the Buffalo River. The top of my little Metropolitan served as a bar on which I mixed martinis while a frog chorus along the river harrumphed its basso profundo. After full dark, the whole valley was sparked by swarms of fireflies.

The evening was a full success, interrupted only by dawn. I had a real Anvil Chorus headache, and Martha's mother threatened to throw her out of the house. This was slightly ridiculous because she was thirty-one years old and had a six-year-old daughter.

I put on a tie and met her mother. We promised to keep the affair down to a roar and things settled down. Martha had married young, but it hadn't worked, and she was now trying to get back into the University of Arkansas. My big mouth kept working and, before I realized it, I had taken over her correspondence course in freshman English. It was mostly themes and essays, taught by a woman named O'Kelly. Without question, it was the most difficult English course I ever encountered, far harder than anything I had found at TCU or the University of Missouri.

We beat O'Kelly for an A and promptly scheduled another martini party for the Valley of the Fireflies. Pat Teague won his election handily, and on election night, we had a sound truck blaring "Happy Days" around the square in Berryville. Teague was especially jubilant because he still hadn't dismounted from his Cadillac for any close contact with the citizenry.

Lacking immediate priorities, I was researching the Kiowa Indians, a once fierce tribe going to seed across the Oklahoma line, when the mayor of Eureka Springs came tromping up the stairs to my apartment one night. He was a retired army colonel who sold real estate. He said that in nine weeks the city was due to host its sixteenth Ozark Folk Festival but was about to cancel because of little interest and no money. "We were wondering if you'd run it for us," the colonel said.

I had never run a folk festival and wasn't even sure I was a folk. He opened the folder he had brought and showed me the civic file on past festivals. I asked him if I would have full control and he said yes.

I glanced through the folder and told him he didn't have enough time left for adequate preparation. They hadn't even booked any headliners. If they'd leave me alone, I would set something up for them, but I had to have a telephone and a secretary. The colonel said they would install me a telephone but had no funds for a secretary or expenses.

In short, Eureka Springs had 1408 residents and a picturesque location and wanted to play the tourist game but could not afford to buy any chips. How did they intend to spread the word? By town crier? The problem was so severe I took it on. That goddamned phone they put in cost me twelve hundred dollars before I was through with it.

Working in the university library in Fayetteville, I used *Editor & Publisher* and other current references to compile the necessary lists. I sent festival announcement releases to all city editors on major papers in Arkansas, Louisiana, Mississippi, Texas, Oklahoma, Kansas, and Missouri. The same release went to most television stations in those states and all radio stations.

The only folk headliner I could find in Arkansas was a singer-songwriter named Jimmy Driftwood, who lived in a small town near Mountain View. I had never met or seen him but his name sounded right. He had been on the Grand Ole Opry a few times, mostly boosting his crossover hit "The Battle of New Orleans," which Johnny Horton's release had made famous. I drove up to see him and found a lanky, taciturn man. He listened to me and said yes, he would like to headline the festival show. In his parlor, he had a six-foot chalk dog listening to His Master's Voice. RCA had given it to him because of the hit song.

That meant a personalized release on Driftwood to all networks and newspapers, especially columnists. Driftwood began to assemble a supporting cast, and the local antique auditorium had to be given sound checks.

My principal allies were the Wheelers, who owned the local weekly newspaper. Everett Wheeler and his family had moved to Eureka Springs from Taos after they found a big brick building for sale with the newspaper franchise. Everett was a master printer, the best I ever saw. He and his diminutive wife worked compulsively to eliminate smudges and typos. Their son Bob, who had been a Marine pilot in Korea, handled layout and graphics. He was also a dab hand at silk-screening.

We flooded our media lists with sprightly brochures of a dancing mountain lass twirling on her sixteenth birthday, who had been drawn for us by a moonlighting artist from Hallmark greeting cards. Podunk radio stations began calling in from seven states. We kept mailing and I kept phoning.

Ten days before our opening, my phone rang at midnight and a brusque eastern voice told me that NBC would be coming down with a ten-man crew to cover our festival. The caller's only inquiry: could I arrange for a cherry-picker to aid in their camera work? With streets as precipitous as ours, they would need it to get the proper angles on our opening parade and the following outdoor scenes.

AND DID THEY COME TO THE FAIR? You betcha. For three days in mid-October, a torrent of outlanders converged on the small Ozark hill town, coming from every state in the US. One party came from Hawaii and several from Europe. Each day for those three days, twenty times Eureka Springs's normal population jammed its streets.

The opening-day parade alone had more participants than the town normally held, including twenty-seven school bands. We lost the famous Budweiser horses and chariots because their wagon-master would not risk his huge Clydesdales on our steep streets. The Tyson chicken company barbecued twelve hundred chickens in a small park to feed these paraders, all on the cuff.

In past years, one of the festival's strongest supporters had been Harry Flowers in his Memphis newspaper column. Someone in Eureka had offended him the year before, and he had brusquely refused our invitation to be a guest of honor. Flowers wrote a highly literate, even classical, column, so I barraged him with letters bursting with Latin, Greek, and old English quotes. He turned up with his magnolia-type wife and churned things up considerably.

I had watched our media hype-ware growing, and added folk arts and crafts exhibits to our stage shows. We had turkey shoots, muzzle-loading rifle contests with molds to pour the contestants' own ammunition, soap-making in huge iron kettles, and flax weaving. We had no hope of housing so many visitors. Overnight accommodations backed up to Rogers, Bentonville, Fayetteville, Harrison, and even Springfield, Missouri.

Jimmy Driftwood, a funereal figure in rusty black, headed a cast of mountain pickers, stompers, and singers, including a couple of yodelers. He could always rouse a cheer with "The Battle of New Orleans" and his next-best-known song, "The Tennessee Stud," and he had some musicians who had appeared before President Kennedy just the month before, in Heber Springs.

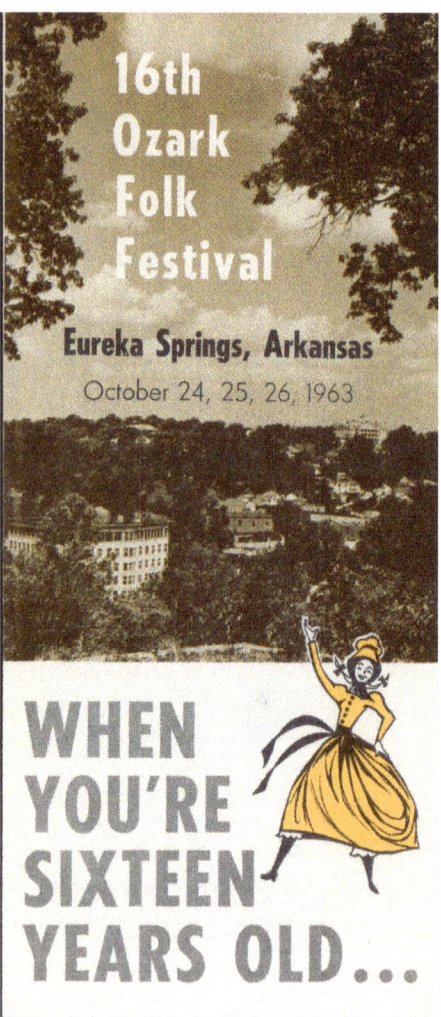

By pure happenstance and having no intention of doing so, Jim Phillips nonetheless found himself in charge of organizing the 16th Annual Ozark Folk Festival, which was a smashing success. *(Author Collection)*

Driftwood had a bad habit which I had also noticed in Hollywood and nightclubs. In addition to being top-billed, he also introduced all the acts. Having done so, he would not leave the stage, creating a deliberate distraction from small acts getting their biggest break. To emphasize the indignity, he wore a red shirt while performing and hovered around the spotlight like an intruding moth.

We got through it. Every merchant in town sold out everything in stock and the twenty-hour days ended for me. After sleeping for a couple of days, I called Martha and asked her to ride to Fayetteville with me. I needed to design a letter of thanks to all the newspapers, radio and television stations, and wire services that had given the festival space or time.

After I had composed the letter, we drove by Collier's drugstore. Still bone-tired, I asked Martha if she wanted me to get her anything. Watching young collegians pushing in and out of the drugstore, I sighed and, always one to rise to the occasion, said, "Well, hell . . ."

The next morning we drove to Henrietta, Oklahoma, and got married.

AFTER MY THIRD MARRIAGE I felt like a surcingled rodeo horse. The careless end of my body had created a new life. Now it was up to my head to provide for it. Thought of the approaching birth turned my Ozark frolic into something serious. As Martha's body swelled, I wondered where the money was going to come from.

I already had a son, Shawn, who was nearly twenty, and I had failed him. Fortunately, he was being cared for by his mother's parents, who were wealthy. But who was to stand surrogate for another child?

Every school day Martha drove a fifty-mile round trip to Fayetteville, where she was enrolled in the University of Arkansas. Every night she worked a full shift as a telephone operator. We had rented a house in Bentonville, where we had a polite neighbor

Left to his own devices, Shawn Phillips went on to become an international music recording artist whose catalog of work includes 19 solo albums as well as collaborations with The Beatles, Donovan, Kansas, and many others. *(Author Collection)*

named Sam Walton. A year before, he had opened his first discount store in Rogers, a few miles away. He called it Wal-Mart.

My employment record proved conclusively that I was a disaster in a corporate setting. The only successes I had enjoyed came when I operated completely solo, and there was little market for my ideas in Arkansas.

That left writing, at which I had once been successful. So I sat down, started writing, and did not stop for fifteen years. I was forty-nine years old, and what came out of the typewriter was a series of twenty-two paperback espionage-adventure books, featuring a freelance spy named Joe Gall. In the process, I traveled to fifty-two foreign countries. The only principal one I missed was the USSR. I tried to make it there, too, but while planning a trip from Moscow to Vladivostok on the Trans-Siberian Railroad, I was told that I would have to buy four first-class tickets to have working room enroute.

The resulting books, printed in several languages, sold nearly fifteen million copies. They capitalized on local backgrounds, native customs, and a convenient current political hook. In a sense, I was just selling real estate, collating the details while I actually lived in the country being portrayed. I nearly got to Antarctica. Working in Christchurch, New Zealand, where the flights to the South Pole originate, I tried to wangle my way down on one of the trips, flashing my old Marine Corps credentials. The authorities were not impressed.

My work methods were unique. I never had a contract and never got a suggestion for any of the stories. In those fifteen years, the editors never knew where I was. Manuscripts kept arriving for them in New York from Addis Ababa, Fremantle, Singapore, and Djibouti. My singular advantage was that when I went to buy a ticket, I knew exactly what accommodations I wanted but didn't give a damn where I was going. What I wanted was single-cabin occupancy on a freighter. Not a cruise ship; in my life I have ridden only two cruise ships. With the exception of flying, they are the poorest way to travel ever invented. But on a freighter operated by a Scandinavian, German, Dutch, English, Canadian, or US line, there is no better environment for a writer. Nineteen times I have gone down the big river from New Orleans on freighters heading everywhere in the world.

The reason I could accept any port of call was the editor in New York who was buying all these sprightly travelogues. Knox Burger had been fiction editor at *Collier's* during the years I was selling them stories. A few times, I had doctored lame stories he had in inventory. After the failure of that magazine, he worked for Dell Publishing, then became chief fiction editor at Fawcett Publications. He remained dubious of my intent to stick with the Joe Gall series but, on the other hand, he kept buying them.

LIAM, MY SECOND SON, was born on schedule. His mother continued commuting to the Fayetteville campus and was duly graduated from the University of Arkansas. At the same time, working a murderous late-night shift, she started moving up in the telephone company and wound up on the managerial level in St. Louis. As usual, I was a delinquent parent during the boy's formative years. His father was a Flying Dutchman, ranging across every sea, rarely home for more than a few months a year.

In trying to compensate for my prolonged absences, I set up overseas holidays for Martha and Liam. When he was five, the target was Grenada, southernmost in the Windward Islands. It lately came into prominence when US foreign policy was being directed by a certain Colonel North. I had been living in the island's small

James Atlee Phillips with son Liam, born November 14, 1964, seen here at Camp Stewart for Boys in Hunt, Texas. A family tradition, all four original Phillips brothers and their sons attended the annual Summer Camp. *(Author Collection)*

country-club house on a nine-hole golf course, finishing a book on the Caribbean area.

Another of those two-week visits was a Christmas celebration in Hong Kong. We had a seventeenth-floor hotel suite in Kowloon overlooking the dazzling harbor and Hong Kong Island. Instead of a Christmas tree, I had some Chinese artisans set up a pink neon dragon twenty feet high. We toured the New Territories, and from Lok Ma Chau we peered into the People's Republic of China.

When he was twelve, Liam got to see a quarter million wild animals in one incredible herd, migrating across the Serengeti Plain. Based in Nairobi at the Norfolk Hotel, we toured seven of the game preserves in a station wagon. Our vehicle was charged by rhinos, and we sighted two leopards. Liam favored the evening stops at lodges, where he could watch elephants spray each other at the water holes.

After we had completed our motor safari of the wild game parks of Kenya and Tanzania, they flew back to the States and I spent three months in Addis Ababa, the high Ethiopian capital. There I got to see an authentic emperor, Haile Selassie, granting audience to his subjects, and marveled at the swaying green tapestries eucalyptus groves made in the long valleys. While working in Addis, I became a card-carrying member of the Robert Kennedy Library, which he had flown over to dedicate.

In 1972, after completing *The Judah Lion Contract*, fourteenth in the Joe Gall series, I was again at liberty to choose a new direction. Although I did not realize it, serendipity was about to fire its best fastball at me. I caught a plane from Addis Ababa to Djibouti and from there a short flight to Aden. My carrier was a venerable DC-3 operated by Brothers Airline. There was a goat grazing in the passenger aisle. He was not a large goat, however, and behaved admirably.

Aden is a seared port which for decades had represented hardship duty for British civil servants. Now it was part of the new Marxist state of South Yemen. The airport authorities looked with obvious hostility at the Western writer who wandered by. After considerable delay, they approved my transit visa and I got a room in the Rock Hotel. It was air-conditioned, a welcome relief from the stifling heat outside.

I asked around at the port offices and the airport, seeking a way out, because I could only stay for forty-eight hours. There were no ships or planes available. Finally, in the lobby of the hotel, a British petroleum engineer told me that the *Vishamn*, a Swedish freighter, had anchored out in the roadstead. He did not know where she was bound or how long she would be in the harbor.

Walking to the nearest dock, I hired a local bum boat to ferry me out to the moored vessel. As we chugged through the slight chop toward her, I noticed that she was old, her hull rusted. She was riding fairly high above the line, so she couldn't have been heavily loaded. No one challenged me as I came aboard, clinging to the gangplank lines. A seaman was working on the first aft hatch cover. When I asked where the captain was, he motioned toward the bridge with his head.

I climbed the flight of stairs and, finding the wheelhouse empty, went on toward the captain's office-cabin. A young man in greasy dungarees was slouched behind the desk, looking dispirited. I was annoyed because I wasn't looking for a junior officer or cadet.

"Like to see the Captain."

The lean young man stared at the leg he had thrown over the corner of the desk. "You're looking at him," he said. His English was distinct, but it was obvious that he was not fully at home in it. I introduced myself and said I was trying to find passage to a European port, any European port. That raised one of his eyebrows. I commented that he looked young to hold skipper rank and asked how long he had been a captain.

"About five hours," he answered. He introduced himself as Per Westerstahl and took a bottle of schnapps from the desk drawer. We each had one and he explained how the freighter came to have a fledgling master in the port of Aden. *Vishamn* had been operated by the Salen line, out of Goteborg, Sweden, for nearly four decades. She had hauled general cargo but was now on her last trip. When she finished this run, she was headed for the breaker's yard, fit only for junk. Her previous captain had become ill, said Westerstahl, so he had been flown in from Hamburg to bring her home. He had been the senior first mate on Salen's officer list and, like most of them, had held a master's ticket for several years.

We had another shot of schnapps and he suggested that I might not want to come aboard because the ship had five ports to make in the Red Sea. Then it would visit Lourenco Marques [now Maputo] and round Africa to several Spanish ports before returning through the Channel to Dutch ports and Hamburg.

I asked him to quote me a price to Hamburg. He rummaged around in his unfamiliar desk but couldn't find any passenger rate sheet and cursed methodically in Swedish. "What do you know about golf?" he asked suddenly.

I told him I had grown up at the edge of a course but hadn't been very good at it. "But you know the rules?" he insisted. When I nodded, he said that he would have his radio man contact Goteborg, requesting permission to take me aboard as a passenger. Ordinarily they didn't carry any but, if Salen would okay it, he would get me the cheapest price in the book.

We had another schnapps, and my flight back down the gangway ladder to the waiting bum boat seemed much easier than my way up. The next day at noon, Captain Westerstahl sent two seamen in the freighter's shore-boat to pick me up. That night we moved across to Djibouti.

Vishamn had once been a fine lady. Like all Scandinavian

ships, she was well-found, and there was no plastic in her. The baroque salon furniture was mahogany. Later, off a stormy Cape of Good Hope, one of the huge chairs got loose and tumbled like an immense bowling ball as the ship nosedived. It had been bolted down but broke loose and required several men to tame it.

From Djibouti, we moved up the Red Sea to Asmara, then back across to Hodeida, principal port of North Yemen. The high capital of that country, Sana'a, was a walled citadel at least a century behind the outside world. As the only passenger but carried on the ship's crew list, I was free to wander while cargo was being worked in port.

Bright-eyed as a gooney bird, I strolled the streets of Port Sudan, where even the dock warehouses look like mosques. The Saudi Arabian port authorities there ruled that no cargo could be unloaded there because, before I joined her, the ship had gone to Haifa, an Israeli port. And that was that. The Arab authorities didn't drink and were too rich to bribe, so I never got to see Mecca and the Kaaba, the small building which holds the sacred Black Stone.

Eager to leave the humid Red Sea, we went booming back to Aden like a Cunard liner, with Chief Engineer Gunnar Thelin cosseting the ship's ancient power plant. She rolled through the Gulf of Aden, and when she was approaching the Horn of Africa, the party began. We had no landfall until Mozambique, and everything was battened down. Captain Westerstahl broke out the ship's spirits and beer and the tarpaulined hatch covers became huge tables, covered with carousing seamen.

We even had a dancing girl, a lissome teenager named Greta, who was traveling with the chief electrician and served as a stewardess. For a day and a night, as the old ship breasted down the east side of Africa, the revel continued. At one point, the bosun approached me and pointed out indignantly that if nothing was done the beer would run out in an hour. I briefed Westerstahl on the matter, and he said that if I paid, he would break out a few more cases. I did, and he did, and astonished camels in the Danakil Desert watched us rollicking south.

The next day the ship was deathly quiet. Per Westerstahl was standing on the fantail as usual, slugging golf balls into his net, but his heart didn't seem in it. Often, an iron shot would miss the net entirely and he would donate another new ball to the Indian Ocean.

Lourenco Marques is one of the loveliest small seaports in the world. Its name is Maputo now, which isn't an improvement. We picked up some pelletized chrome there for delivery in Barcelona. The Cape of Good Hope can blow nearly as hard as the Horn, and for a day, she threatened to sink the ship before we could deliver her to the breakers.

In Barcelona, I walked the Ramblas again, and took Westerstahl and Gunnar Thelin to some of the fine cafes. Malaga saw us for three days, then Cadiz, which is just around Gibraltar, and another week to Antwerp. Then Hamburg, and we all walked away from the condemned ship.

WHERE IN THE WORLD HAVE I BEEN? From the wing of the bridge deck on a tossing ship I have passed through Sunda Strait, where Krakatoa erupted. I have watched the fabled kiwi bird faint when presented to public view. I've walked the New Zealand forest where men long ago killed each other for a pound of tree resin which was worth more than gold. I've felt my heart quicken at the rough, misty beauty of the Dingle Peninsula in the west of Ireland. I've bowed my head in Istanbul's Blue Mosque.

I completed the twenty-second book of the Joe Gall series aboard a Lykes Lines freighter standing off Saigon. In our holds were ten thousand tons of rice for the Vietnamese capital, corrupted by years of unwinnable war. While we waited for permission to enter through a narrow riverine approach open to enfilading fire, the U.S. Embassy began its helicopter evacuation. The year was 1975.

As our freighter returned to Singapore to unload the rice, I finished the series, having my protagonist resign from his intelligence agency. It seemed the proper time for it.

Were the books any good? I couldn't tell. For nearly fifteen years, I had been working on them all over the world, sweeping up the kitchen, cannibalizing my previous work, adapting to the new vistas unreeling before me. In *20th Century Crime & Mystery Writers*, a standard reference work, a critic named R. Jeff Banks passed this judgment: "His achievement in this series may well be regarded by future historians as the best American espionage series of the latter half of the 20th century."

The defense rests. Time to sit down and shut up. Room must be made for new self-appointed gurus spouting passionate nonsense.

ALTHOUGH I DID NOT KNOW IT at the time, the real spy in our family was also retiring. When I decided to terminate the Joe Gall series after twenty-two books, my younger brother, David Atlee Phillips, was resigning from the CIA in Washington after what in his memoir, *The Night Watch*, he called "twenty-five years of peculiar service." He was chief of clandestine services for the Western hemisphere and had reached the highest rating in the CIA possible without presidential appointment.

During the years my clownish protagonist had been masquerading around the world, Dave had been turning over real shithouses, with real people in them. In 1954, he had been a principal in throwing Jacobo Árbenz out of Guatemala, a precedent which led to the disasters in El Salvador and Nicaragua. He handled propaganda broadcasts during the Bay of Pigs invasion, and personally talked General Elias Wessin into leaving the Dominican Republic when we shuffled administrations there. In 1982, when U.S. Marines swarmed ashore in Lebanon, Dave was waiting for them.

His work and the fact that I was writing a fictional series on espionage obviously posed problems. I had resolved them by not seeing or communicating with him for fifteen years, making it impossible to use, even inadvertently, any material I might have learned from the connection.

The only time Dave and I had spent together on a familiar basis was a few weeks in New York in the late '40s, while we were helping our mother die of cancer. At the time, he still had theatrical aspirations and made all the cattle calls. We lived in the same apartment, and I gradually came to realize that he was a swordsman with quite a following.

The only lasting impression I have of this period is a throwaway anecdote about one of his difficult conquests. While a student at William and Mary, he had pursued a campus beauty for a long time without success. She was engaged, and determined not to share the wealth with him. They finally reached an agreement. He could have her, completely and carnally, but only while she was talking on the telephone to her fiance. She was actually on the phone with her betrothed while David humped her.

As the years passed and his undercover importance grew, I slowly became aware that my passport was being subjected to closer scrutinies. Foreign security officials in airports and ports lingered before admitting me, faces altering slightly when they glanced at my name, passport picture, and face. More and more often they consulted lists in inner offices. Once, in the People's Republic of South Yemen, I thought they weren't going to admit me at all.

After Saigon fell, I looked forward to a day when we would open a bottle of sour mash and discuss where our travels might have intersected. In 1980, when I was living in a suburban townhouse in St. Louis, he flew in to address a downtown convention. For years, he had moonlighted as a lecturer.

The man I picked up at the St. Louis airport had more history in his face than the younger brother I remembered. There was sufficient reason for the change. He had bailed out of a burning bomber in World War Two and had been directing subterranean violence all over the world since then. What had been an almost pretty boy had become a granitic man, so reserved he seemed carved from stone.

He stayed with us overnight, and we split a bottle. He was affable, but there was no time for private conversation. He was drinking by the numbers, had obviously been doing so for a long time, and smoked constantly. But he never slurred a syllable or stopped listening to the wind blow outside. The next morning I drove him to the downtown hotel where he was to speak and afterward to the airport.

The next night, thinking of all the subjects we had not covered, I realized it was the first time in thirty years I knew where he was on a given night. I called his Pittsburgh hotel room. He answered promptly and assured me he was fine.

We talked a few times after that but without heat. Our politics were so different we had long ago given up any attempt at reconciling our views. There was only one sharp exchange. He called to say that he and the agency were filing a lawsuit against an author who was trying to place him in Dallas at the time of the Kennedy assassination. Another proposed book was trying to link him to the Letelier car-bombing deaths in Washington.

Since I knew nothing of the facts involved, I murmured a meaningless answer. At the other end of the line, from his Bethesda study, he exploded suddenly. "Goddammit!" he shouted. "You never comment!"

"Whoa, now. If you want to discuss the car-bombing, you seem to have a connection. You lived in Chile a long time, owned a newspaper there. You called the shots on the operation when Allende died. I was watching television in a Buenos Aires hotel room when that happened. I saw the fighters strafing his presidential palace. So there is a Chilean connection."

I waited, but no sound came from the telephone receiver at my ear.

"As for the Dallas identity, I've known you awhile. That possibility is plain goddamned silly."

He finally answered. "But you defend that goddamned Ramsey Clark." He was referencing the former Attorney General and longtime New Frontiersman.

"That's bullshit too. I don't know Mr. Clark. If it comes to that, I don't know you very well. I defend Mr. Clark's *position* on certain subjects. Dissent is not treason."

We had a silent line again. Finally he said, in a tired voice: "I love you."

Six weeks later, my lawyer brother in Fort Worth phoned to tell me that David had inoperable terminal lung cancer. A few days afterward,

David called and said that he was going through some of the chemical foolishness because it would make his family more comfortable.

"Right," I said. "I'll be seeing you."

I didn't linger on his demise because I knew he had carried the solution to such problems for years and would use it when he was ready. They gave him a formal burial at Arlington. William Colby, former director of the CIA, thanked his coffin for a grateful nation.

James Atlee Phillips (top left), Olcott Phillips (top right), David Atlee Phillips (bottom right), and Edwin Phillips (bottom left). *(Author Collection)*

HAVING COMPLETED A JOURNEY of seventy-five years, I am a white Anglo-Saxon male who never represented anyone but himself. People in almost every country in the world will say yes, he passed by here. Why? What was he seeking? He didn't say. A commercially successful writer who roamed without a contract, he was an intelligent and arrogant man who was married three times but never let social events interrupt his travels.

The time period of these peregrinations was 1915 to 1990. When the journey began, Woodrow Wilson was in the White House, and no woman could vote. There was no television and no scheduled aircraft travel, and the automobile was new. Things have indeed, changed: some for better, some for worse. Peering into the world's back yards, I was an impartial observer of both affairs of state and the going price of used baby carriages. There is a connection.

TIME TO SAY GOOD-NIGHT NOW. Death, as in the Irish legend, will soon be coming silently up the back stairway. There are good things to remember. Donald Douglas's DC-3 plane. Citizen Ralph Nader, fighting for the common safety. Flying Cloud, the clipper ship designed by Donald McKay of Boston, spanking along with a bone in her teeth, three-quarters of an acre of canvas set . . .

It can be dark on the Armageddon road, and the heralds of despair are numerous. Great care must be taken to examine their credentials. Here two questions must be asked: Was it a record of what happened to Colombia's nation from 1915 to 1990? Or is it only what happened to Colombia herself?

While I was meditating just now, in the Texas port where I now live, the talking furniture announced that a Category Five hurricane, bearing winds of 175 miles an hour, was approaching. I may be moving again.

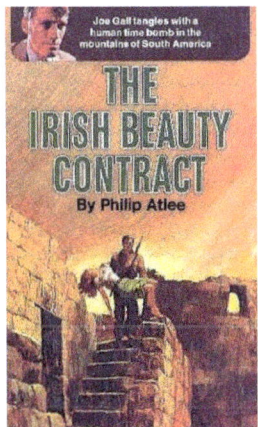
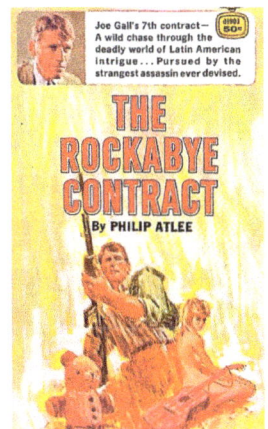
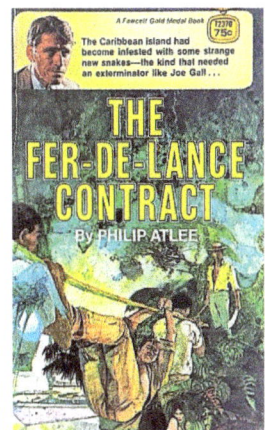

Covers for the Contract series featuring various artworks. *(Free Use/Public Domain)*

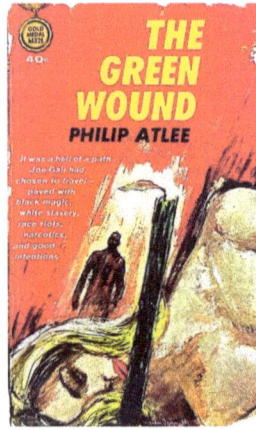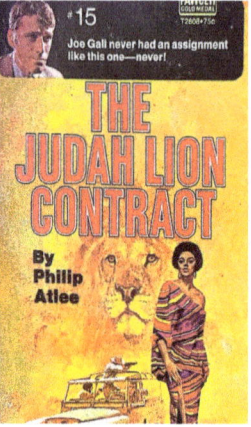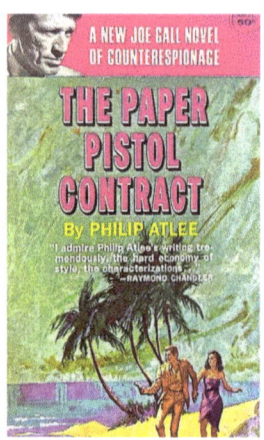
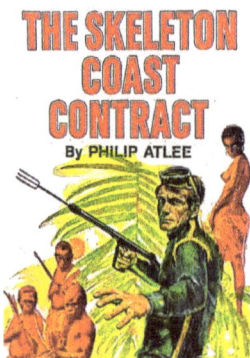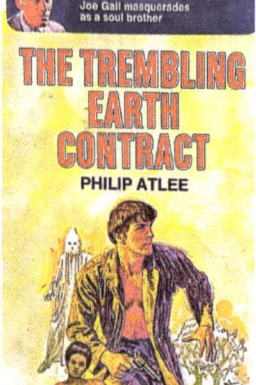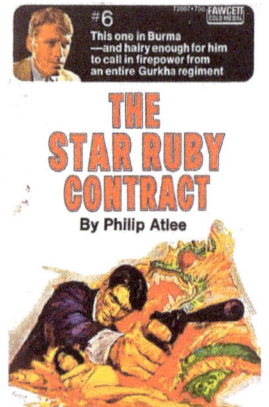
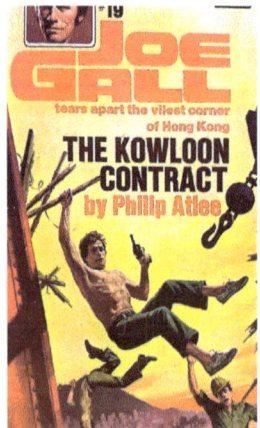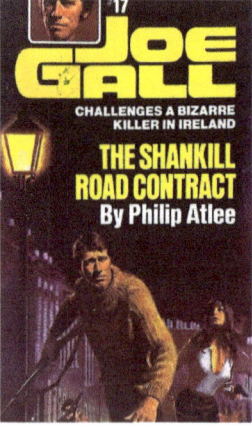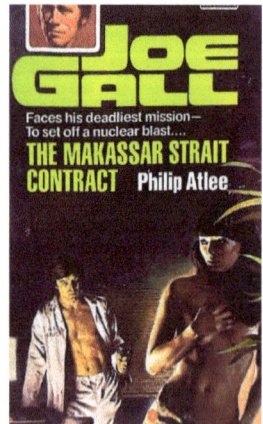

Covers for the Contract series featuring various artworks. *(Free Use/Public Domain)*

ACKNOWLEDGMENTS

The author would like to thank:

My wife, Martha Phillips, for her undying love and support.

Francis Nevins, author, editor, critic, friend, believer, and astute interrogator.

Liam Phillips and the Phillips family would like to express their sincere thanks to all who made the publication of this memoir possible, including:

Jim Donovan—author, editor, advisor, friend, and literary agent extraordinaire—for his professionalism, candor, humor, and incredible know-how. This book truly would not exist without him. The Nullifier owes you.

Lisa and Atlee Phillips, for love, laughter, and absolute support every step of the way.

Beth Phillips, daughter of Edwin Phillips, for her undying enthusiasm, invaluable custodianship of the Phillips Family records and photographs, and perpetual good humor.

Shawn Phillips, number-one son, for his patience, understanding, insight, and love.

J.R. and Lynn Andrade (née Phillips) for their love, encouragement, and support.

Patricia Everett, Editorial Production Coordinator, *Leatherneck—Magazine of the Marines*. Your kindness and enthusiastic optimism made a real difference.

Sara Pezzoni, Photo Collections Coordinator at the UTA Libraries. Thank you for knowing how it all works and having the patience to explain it to me.

Carol McKenzie, transcriptionist bar none.

Special thanks must also be given to everyone at TCU Press for their patience, professionalism, and hard work, including, but not limited to: Dan Williams, Marco Roc, Adrienne Martinez, James Lehr, and Abigail Jennings.

BIBLIOGRAPHY

James Young Phillips, AKA, James Atlee Phillips, AKA, Philip Atlee

Short Stories and Novellas

As James Young Phillips

1. Phillips, James Young. "Tennessee Tornado." *Scholastic*, 1942.

As James Atlee Phillips:

2. Phillips, James Atlee. "Hero Weather." *Saturday Evening Post*, March 3, 1942.
3. Phillips, James Atlee. "Report Unfounded." *Collier's*, July 3, 1943.
4. Phillips, James Atlee. "Lend Lease Christmas Tree." *Collier's*, January 1, 1944.
5. Phillips, James Atlee. "First Blood." *Collier's*, July 7, 1945.
6. Phillips, James Atlee. "The Acing of Field Marshal Cluff." *Adventure*, December 1945 (Reprint, *Adventure*, April 1961).
7. Phillips, James Atlee. "Chicken is Just a Bird." *AM Magazine*, January 1946.
8. Phillips, James Atlee. "The Kunming Story." *Adventure*, February 1946.
9. Phillips, James Atlee. "Delegate from Everywhere." *Scholastic*, May 6, 1946.
10. Phillips, James Atlee. "The Master Stroke." *Liberty*, October 19, 1946.
11. Phillips, James Atlee. "Make It Look Good." *Collier's*, November 23, 1946.
12. Phillips, James Atlee. "Father Sanchez and the Bull." *Liberty*, December 21, 1946.
13. Phillips, James Atlee. "Ambassador to the Human Race." *Esquire*, November 1947.
14. Phillips, James Atlee. "Jackal Song." *Adventure*, June 1948.
15. Phillips, James Atlee. "Chousey Man" (w/Biographical Sketch). *Collier's*, July 31, 1948.
16. Phillips, James Atlee. "Saturday Fever." *Collier's*, October 16, 1948.
17. Phillips, James Atlee. "Final Bell." *Collier's*, November 13, 1948.
18. Phillips, James Atlee. "Just Like I Hate Money." *Collier's*, July 23, July 30, 1949.

19. Phillips, James Atlee. "Moulmein Star." *Collier's*, December 31, 1949.
20. Phillips, James Atlee. "Substitute Star." *Collier's*, July 22, 1950.
21. Phillips, James Atlee. "Trick and Fancy." *Collier's*, January 13, 1951.
22. Phillips, James Atlee. "Run for the Money." *Collier's*, October 20, 1951.
23. Phillips, James Atlee. "Brass Lullaby." *Collier's*, March 1, 1952.
24. Phillips, James Atlee. "The Moonshine Bull." *Argosy*, March 1952.
25. Phillips, James Atlee. "Master of the Manse." *Collier's*, May 10, 1952.
26. Phillips, James Atlee. "Fast Break." *Argosy*, May 1952.
27. Phillips, James Atlee. "Vendetta." *Collier's*, July 12, 1952.
28. Phillips, James Atlee. "Love Set." *Collier's*, July 26, 1952.
29. Phillips, James Atlee and F.H. Young. "A Fathom of Pearls." *Collier's*, August 23, 1952.
30. Phillips, James Atlee. "No Room at the Inn." *Cosmopolitan*, December 1952.
31. Phillips, James Atlee. "Big Rig." *Nations Business*, February 1953.
32. Phillips, James Atlee. "File and Forget." *Cosmopolitan*, April 1953.
33. Phillips, James Atlee. "Deadly Mermaid." *Collier's*, June 27, July 4, July 11, 1953.
34. Phillips, James Atlee. "He Put Violence Aside." *Nation's Business*, October 1953.
35. Phillips, James Atlee. "Condition: Critical." *Argosy*, January 1954.
36. Phillips, James Atlee. "The Wife Who Lived Twice." *Collier's*, February 19, 1954.
37. Phillips, James Atlee. "Comeback." *Saturday Evening Post*, September 18, 1954.
38. Phillips, James Atlee. "Worthless Young Man." *The Saturday Evening Post*, March 15, 1958.
39. Phillips, James Atlee. "The Generation Gap." *Argosy*, November 1967.

Poetry

1. Phillips, James Atlee. "The Metal Forest." Published by author, circa 1940-42.
2. Phillips, James Atlee. "Sand, Wind, and Stars." N.p., circa 1940-42.

Articles for *Leatherneck*, The Official Magazine of the Marine Corps

1. Phillips, James Atlee. "Revolution by Radar." *Leatherneck*, November 1945.
2. Phillips, James Atlee. "The Man from Everywhere." *Leatherneck*, December 1945.
3. Phillips, James Atlee. "Blind Date in Jersey." *Leatherneck*, January 1946.
4. Phillips, James Atlee. "A Marine Comes Home." *Leatherneck*, February 1946.
5. Phillips, James Atlee. "The Cradle of the Corps." *Leatherneck*, March 1946.

6. Phillips, James Atlee. "The Saddle Sergeant." *Leatherneck*, March 1946.
7. Phillips, James Atlee. "Sucker Punch." *Leatherneck*, April 1946.
8. Phillips, James Atlee. "Pacific Dream." *Leatherneck*, May 1946.
9. Phillips, James Atlee. "Phantom Marine." *Leatherneck*, May 1946.
10. Phillips, James Atlee. "The Orchid Bomber." *Leatherneck*, June 1946.
11. Phillips, James Atlee. "Operation Smokey." *Leatherneck*, June 1946.
12. Phillips, James Atlee. "Hank Adams Changes Beats." *Leatherneck*, October 1946.
13. Phillips, James Atlee. "Combat Camp." *Leatherneck*, November 1946.
14. Phillips, James Atlee. "El Toro Marine Air Station." *Leatherneck*, February 1947.

Novels

As Philip Atlee:

Atlee, Philip. *The Inheritors*. Dial Press, 1940.

As James Atlee Phillips:

1. Phillips, James Atlee. *The Case of the Shivering Chorus Girls*. 1942.
2. Phillips, James Atlee. *Suitable for Framing*. 1950.
3. Phillips, James Atlee. *Pagoda*. 1951.
4. Phillips, James Atlee. *The Deadly Mermaid*. 1954.

Then resuming as Philip Atlee:

The Contract Series, Featuring, Joe Gall, The Nullifier
(All published by Gold Medal)

1. Atlee, Philip. *The Green Wound* (reprinted as *The Green Wound Contract*). Gold Medal, 1963.
2. Atlee, Philip. *The Silken Baroness* (reprinted as *The Silken Baroness Contract*). Gold Medal, 1966.
3. Atlee, Philip. *The Death Bird Contract*. Gold Medal, 1966.
4. Atlee, Philip. *The Paper Pistol Contract*. Gold Medal, 1966.
5. Atlee, Philip. *The Irish Beauty* Contract. Gold Medal, 1966.
6. Atlee, Philip. *The Star Ruby* Contract. Gold Medal, 1967.
7. Atlee, Philip. T*he Rockabye* Contract. Gold Medal, 1968.
8. Atlee, Philip. *The Skeleton Coast Contract*. Gold Medal, 1968.
9. Atlee, Philip. *The Ill Wind Contract*. Gold Medal, 1969.

10. Atlee, Philip. *The Trembling Earth Contract.* Gold Medal, 1969.
11. Atlee, Philip. *The Fer-de-Lance Contract.* Gold Medal, 1971.
12. Atlee, Philip. *The Canadian Bomber Contract.* Gold Medal, 1971.
13. Atlee, Philip. *The White Wolverine Contract.* Gold Medal, 1971.
14. Atlee, Philip. *The Kiwi Contract.* Gold Medal, 1972.
15. Atlee, Philip. *The Judah Lion Contract.* Gold Medal, 1973.
16. Atlee, Philip. *The Spice Route Contract.* Gold Medal, 1973.
17. Atlee, Philip. *The Shankill Road Contract.* Gold Medal, 1973.
18. Atlee, Philip. *The Underground Cities Contract.* Gold Medal, 1974.
19. Atlee, Philip. *The Kowloon Contract.* Gold Medal, 1974.
20. Atlee, Philip. *The Black Venus Contract.* Gold Medal, 1975.
21. Atlee, Philip. *The Makassar Strait Contract.* Gold Medal, 1976.
22. Atlee, Philip. *The Last Domino Contract.* Gold Medal, 1976.

Also included in the following compilations:

1. Atlee, Philip. "The Inheritors." In *Roundup Time: A Collection of Southwestern Writing.* Whittlesey House, 1943.
2. Phillips, James A. "First Blood." In *Western Stories Selected by Gene Autry.* Dell Books, 1947.
3. Phillips, James Atlee. "Fast Break." In *The Argosy Book of Sports Stories.* Barnes Publications, April 1953.

Screenplays and Treatments

1. *The Plymouth Adventure,* written by James Atlee Phillips, MGM, 1951.
2. *Big Jim McLain,* written by James Edward Grant, Richard English (original story), Eric Taylor (original story), & James Atlee Phillips, directed by Edward Ludwig, featuring John Wayne, Nancy Olson, James Arness, and Alan Napier, released August 30, 1952.
3. *Thunder Road,* written by James Atlee Phillips, Walter Wise, and Robert Mitchum (original story), directed by Arthur Ripley, featuring Robert Mitchum, Gene Barry, Jacques Aubuchon, Keely Smith, and James Mitchum, released May 10, 1958.
4. *Rockabye!,* written by James Atlee Phillips (treatment) and Lawrence Turman, 1965.

Adaptations

1. *Studio One*, season 4, episode 22, "Pagoda," written by James Atlee Phillips (original story), Joseph Liss, and Fletcher Markle, directed by Franklin J. Schaffner, featuring John Forsythe, Betty Furness, and Sono Osato, aired February 11, 1952.
2. *Fireside Theatre*, season 7, episode 8, "The Wife Who Lived Twice," written by James Atlee Phillips (original story) and David Lord, directed by Frank Wisbar, featuring Guillermo Baretto, Alma Beltran, and John Hudson, aired October 26, 1954.
3. *Schlitz Playhouse*, season 4, episode 25, "Fast Break," written by James Atlee Phillips (original story), Sidney Biddell, and DeWitt Bodeen, directed by Justus Addiss, featuring Sebastian Cabot, Jackie Cooper, and Betty Lynn, aired February 25, 1955.

Final Interview

Phillips, James Atlee. "Interview with James Atlee Phillips." Interview by Francis M. Nevins, Jr. *Espionage Magazine*, November 1985.

ABOUT THE AUTHOR

James Young Phillips, pseudonym "Philip Atlee," was a Fort Worth native whose first novel so scandalized the well-to-do citizens of his Country Club upbringing that it was banned from public library shelves. Following stints as a flight dispatcher, Marine, Broadway publicist, and screenwriter, he turned to writing mystery and espionage novels, ultimately selling millions of copies worldwide.

www.ingramcontent.com/pod-product-compliance
Lightning Source LLC
Chambersburg PA
CBHW042146160426
43202CB00023B/2989